MW01200098

KATHY VINTSON

ABUNDANT LIFE IN A CHAOTIC WORLD

the crown effect

Ambassador International
GREENVILLE, SOUTH CAROLINA & BELFAST, NORTHERN IRELAND

www.ambassador-international.com

The Crown Effect

Abundant Life in a Chaotic World
©2024 by Kathy Vinston
All rights reserved

ISBN: 978-1-64960-590-0, hardcover
ISBN: 978-1-64960-430-9, paperback
eISBN: 978-1-64960-478-1
Library of Congress Control Number: 2024931739

Cover Design by Hannah Linder Designs
Interior Typesetting by Dentelle Design
Edited by Kimberly Davis

Scripture taken from the Holy Bible, New International Version®, NIV® Copyright ©1973, 1978, 1984, 2011 by Biblica, Inc.® Used by permission. All rights reserved worldwide.

AMBASSADOR INTERNATIONAL
Emerald House Group, Inc.
411 University Ridge, Suite B14
Greenville, SC 29601
United States
www.ambassador-international.com

AMBASSADOR BOOKS
The Mount
2 Woodstock Link
Belfast, BT6 8DD
Northern Ireland, United Kingdom
www.ambassadormedia.co.uk

The colophon is a trademark of Ambassador, a Christian publishing company.

Dedicated in loving memory of my mammaw, Fannie Mae Statum, who provided me a loving home, taught me about grace, and introduced me to my godly inheritance. She is the reason I wear my crown.

TABLE OF CONTENTS

ACKNOWLEDGMENTS

To my husband, Danny—thank you for being the perfect man for me, supporting me when I suddenly decided to retire and write a book, making me feel beautiful every day, and giving me the family I always dreamed of having.

To my son, Connor, and my daughter, Brittany—thank you for bringing me more joy than I ever dreamed possible and teaching me what it means to love someone more than life itself.

To my daughter-in-law, Haley—you are everything I prayed you would be and more. Thank you for choosing to become one of us and for giving me the two most beautiful granddaughters.

To my granddaughters, Kinsley Grace and Halstyn Kate—thank you for giving me a reason to be the godly example for you that my grandmother was for me. Never forget you were created by God for a purpose.

To my brother, Frank Statum—you are an amazing example of God's grace and what He will do in our lives if we choose Him. I am so proud of you and the amazing family you have raised.

INTRODUCTION

IT WAS A BEAUTIFUL MORNING. I put on a new dress, feeling good about myself, and headed to church with my family. A typical Sunday, we would all attend church and then have lunch at a nearby restaurant. As usual, we were late, so we entered at the top of the balcony and headed down the stairs to find a seat. And that is when it happened—I fell.

Well, I did not actually fall. I missed a step and would have tumbled down fifty more, had I not reached out to catch myself with the handrail. The force was so hard it nearly dislocated my shoulder, but I held fast, dangling in my new dress and clinging to that handrail for my very life. In a matter of seconds, I went from feeling great about myself and life in general to an attitude of indignant shame at having just shown my underwear to everyone in the church balcony. When I looked up, I could see only my sweet, understanding daughter, staring down at me and shaking in silent, hysterical laughter. Unable to pull myself up, I continued to hang for what seemed like forever.

And there you have it—a metaphor for the chaotic life of a modern woman who thinks she has it all together, head held high, until she suddenly finds herself dangling upside down, holding on for dear life, and scrambling to figure out (in no particular order) how she will recover, how she can right herself, why this happened to her, and what she could have done to prevent it. I have a feeling you can relate.

Hopefully, you have never found yourself suspended from a handrail, dress-over-head, during the Sunday morning song service; however, you may feel at times that your life has turned upside down, and you cannot find yourself in the chaos. You do not recognize yourself anymore or do not like the person you have become. Maybe you are burdened with guilt or regret, feeling like you do not measure up, and the burden is more than you can bear. You wonder if God sees you, hears you, or even cares.

I am here to tell you that He does see you, and He does care. He knew life after the Garden of Eden would be chaotic, and He prepared a way for you—a way to a beautiful life amidst the chaos. Jesus said, "'I am the way, and the truth, and the life'" (John 14:6). The moment you accepted Jesus Christ as your Savior, you were born again and began a new life in Christ. You became a child of God and, as His child, you are His heir. Romans 8:16-17 says, "The Spirit himself testifies with our spirit that we are God's children. Now if we are children, then we are heirs—heirs of God and co-heirs with Christ, if indeed we share in his sufferings in order that we may also share in his glory."

You are a daughter of the King. Everything that belongs to God belongs to you because you belong to Him. You are part of His family through your faith in Jesus Christ, and He has given you a promise of an eternal inheritance. Revelation 21:4 provides a beautiful description: "He will wipe every tear from their eyes. There will be no more death or mourning or crying or pain, for the old order of things has passed away."

Oh, how I look forward to the fulfillment of His promise, when I claim my eternal inheritance and spend forever in Heaven with my Father, where no chaos exists! In the meantime, I am here—upside down, holding on, and closing my eyes, so no one can see me. I wonder if my life will truly end, should I bump down the long flight of stairs, as the choir sings "Nearer, My God, to Thee." Reasonably sure the pastor just asked everyone to lift their hands toward the balcony and pray, I wonder about finding a church whose people do not possess the knowledge that I wear granny panties.

The predicament leads to the reason I wrote this book—no, not the indisputable wonders of granny panties (although I am certain that one would be a bestseller). This book is about the profound effect your inheritance will have on your life if you choose to accept and believe all God has for you now, right now, in the middle of the chaos. You see, your inheritance is not held in trust until the moment you leave this world. It is available to you the moment you accept Jesus Christ as your Savior. At that moment, God provides everything you need to overcome chaos, succeed in life, walk in peace, and live an abundant life. But it is not enough to just receive it. You have to actually believe it. The apostle Paul wrote, "As God's co-workers we urge you not to receive God's grace in vain" (2 Cor. 6:1).

The grace of God includes more than just the promise of eternal life. His grace gives you unconditional love, unearned help, unmerited favor, and undeserved peace. It transforms your desires, behaviors, and motivations, giving strength and power to live triumphantly in this world. His grace can change every aspect of your life. But it will not if you receive it "in vain," as Paul said, nor if you do not truly believe all God says about you, all God says He will do, and all God says about living your best life in Him and through Him. Paul continues by saying, "Now is the time of God's favor, now is the day of salvation" (2 Cor. 6:2). God wants to bless you and pour His favor on you now, right in the middle of your messy, hectic life.

In the next few chapters, I am going to share some funny, sad, crazy, and embarrassing stories about my own chaotic life. I do not share them because I am famous, rich, or perfect. Remember, I am still hanging by a handrail, flashing the church congregation. I share these stories simply because, looking back at all the chaos, failures, and falls (no pun intended), I can see the profound effect God's grace has on my life. I can see how my inheritance provides everything I have needed to overcome, but it did so only because I believed. As you read this book, I pray you discover and believe all God says about who you are. I pray you shake off what holds you back and believe you are worthy of all God has planned for you. I pray you allow His light to overcome the darkness of this world and that you claim your godly inheritance as your own, receiving everything you need to live life abundantly. I pray you experience the profound effect His grace can and will have on your life.

Now, that grace does not insure you against chaos or finding your world turned upside down. Remember me? I am still hanging onto this handrail like my life depends on it (which, apparently, it does). But it does mean God will see you, He will hear you, He will care, and He will "meet all your needs according to the riches of his glory in

Christ Jesus" (Phil. 4:19). I trust He will supply everything I need to pull myself up from this handrail before they send the elders of the church to rescue me!

Pause for Reflection

Have you ever felt lost in the chaos, wondering if God cares?

"'My grace is sufficient for you, for my power is made perfect in weakness.' Therefore I will boast all the more gladly about my weaknesses, so that Christ's power may rest on me."

2 Corinthians 12:9

Write what the following phrases mean to you.

Sufficient grace: _____

_____

_____

_____

My power is made perfect in weakness: _____

_____

_____

_____

Christ's power may rest in me: _____

_____

_____

_____

_____

How does this verse apply to you when life turns upside down? ____

_____

_____

_____

_____

When do you feel the most powerful? _____

_____

_____

_____

When does God say you are the most powerful? _____

_____

_____

_____

_____

How might this perspective influence the way you respond when chaos ensues? _____

_____

_____

_____

Write about a time when you felt spiritually weak in a battle. _____

_____

_____

_____

_____

_____

_____

_____

"For we do not have a high priest who is unable to empathize with our weaknesses, but one who has been tempted in every way, just as we are—yet he did not sin. Let us then approach God's throne of grace with confidence, so that we may receive mercy and find grace to help us in our time of need."

Hebrews 4:15-16

How can Jesus identify with our weaknesses? _____

_____

_____

_____

_____

Does this fact make you feel more confident that you will receive His grace: His love, help, favor, and peace in times of need? _____

_____

_____

_____

_____

CHAPTER 1

Know Who You Are

I HEAR VOICES. THERE, I said it—I hear voices. You did not see that one coming, did you? Now, fear not. I am sure I need counseling, but it would not be over the voices in my head. I hear the voices of the enemy telling lies. I battle them every day. No, I do not just battle; I am at war with them. I am in a daily, all-out, fists up, punch Satan in the face kind of war over the asinine, negative voices in my head! I know they are lies. In John 8:44, Jesus Himself said Satan "is a liar and the father of lies." But still I battle, and I have a feeling you battle, too, as you hear the same negative voices trying to tear you down. It is Satan's way of convincing you to wear his brands.

Speaking of brands, I have a confession to make. I have a large closet—a large, pink, customized closet, organized by season, style, and color. I love clothes and shoes. And what is a great outfit without the perfect pair of sunglasses? Surprisingly, among all this customized, organized, categorized fashion, you will not find many designer brands, despite my dedication to the iconic looks of the eighties.

As a teenager, I longed to wear the most popular, expensive brands but never did because we could not afford them. After repeatedly sitting through my grandfather's lecture on the proper amount of toilet paper one should use per bathroom visit, one knew not to ask for luxuries. (In case you are unaware, the appropriate quantity is four squares, two times, for a total of eight squares per visit. One could only hope for two-ply.) Truthfully, most of our clothing came from the thrift store. I do remember scoring a pink Izod polo as a freshman in high school. It was my favorite shirt, and, no doubt, I wore it way too often. Needless to say, I did not make the senior *Who's Who* list for best dressed. Actually, I did not make the list at all. How ironic is it that I remember I did not make that list, but I cannot tell you one person who did? So often, we worry over things that have absolutely no relevance to our true identity and what our future holds.

When I was a young woman and could afford some luxuries without limits on toilet paper squares, I found myself buying the labels for my children and getting by with little for myself. An amazing secret every woman should know is how many days she can go unnoticed for wearing the same pair of black pants. Besides, black definitely makes you look smaller from behind, so you get two times the benefit. My children wore designer brands; I wore black pants.

Now, as a somewhat older woman (I say *somewhat* because the definition of *old* changes every time I enter a new decade), with adult, gainfully employed children who buy their own clothes, I am more interested in how clothing looks on my somewhat-older body than in who designed it. I do not care who you are—if you can design something in a color that brings out my eyes and makes me look thinner, I am buying! I will wear nearly any brand out there, as long as I like it, and it fits, with one exception—Satan's brands.

Satan's brands have nothing to do with logos or monetary value. They are merely a bunch of lies and the effects of those lies on your self-worth. First Peter 5:8 says, "Be alert and of sober mind. Your enemy the devil prowls around like a roaring lion looking for someone to devour." Satan is a liar, and he wants to brand you by making you believe things about yourself that are not true.

He started with me when I was only five years old. My parents had divorced, and my brother and I lived with our mother. One night, when we returned from an evening out with Dad, my mother met us at the door and told him she did not want us anymore. "Take them and let your mother raise them!" she cried.

Of course, my five-year-old self did not understand what was happening. All I knew was that my mother was gone. The woman who had given me life, nourished me, and taken care of me since birth had vanished. Unaware of what she was going through or the horrible childhood she endured, I had no idea she was lost, desperate, and suicidal. The moment my mother gave me up, Satan started trying to brand me, whispering, "You are abandoned."

I sat on my grandmother's sofa for hours, rocking, banging my head on the back cushion, hearing those voices, and wondering what would happen to me, where my mother was, and if I would ever see her again. I rocked until I finally just leaned over and fell asleep. The doctor said my behavior was harmless, and I would outgrow it. The only true physical damage was to my hair, which stayed in knots from the constant head-banging until it had to be cut off, pixie-style.

My beautiful, long, thick, head of hair now barely reached below my ears—evidence of my pain.

Cue the voices: *You are ugly.* We started to visit our mother. No schedule was set; we simply went for an overnight or weekend visit sometimes and continued to live with our dad and grandparents. I can honestly say that my dad really loved me, and I thought he was the greatest man on earth. He was not a big man, barely standing five foot four, but he was athletic and muscular. I remember holding on to his biceps with both hands, while he swung me around until we were both so dizzy that we could barely stand.

I started noticing that he would leave for the evening after those fun, playful times. Then the playing stopped completely because he was not around anymore, and I realized he had a drinking problem. My dad was an alcoholic. He would stop at the bar after work, staggering drunk through the door, if he came home at all. My grandmother and I would pick him up in the middle of the night when he was too drunk to drive home. I remember lying in bed at night, crying and praying for my dad. I was terrified he would die in an accident or be killed in a bar.

Eventually, he remarried in a small family wedding at my grandparents' home. I was a flower girl, but what I remember most is standing in the front yard, waving as they drove away, smiling and pretending to be happy, so no one could see the crushing pain in my heart. My dad left to start over with his new wife and her children, while my brother and I stayed behind to live with our grandparents. Cue the voices: *He does not care about you. He loves his new wife and her children more than you. You are rejected.*

My grandfather was more than willing to take us into his home. Pawpaw could build anything, and he taught my brother everything he knew. They were very close. Our relationship was different. He was our provider; but every time he bought me something, he would pull me aside and say, "Now, you're going to be Pawpaw's buddy, aren't you?" He did not have to explain further—I knew exactly what he meant. I am forever grateful that he never forced himself on me and that I was strong enough to resist his coercion, but I was left unprotected from the way his inappropriate advances and unwelcome words made me feel. The voices in my head echoed, *You are dirty. You should be ashamed.*

When bad things happen, the enemy tries to brand you with his lies. He came after me from a young age with brands like *abandoned*, *ugly*, *rejected*, and *ashamed*; but I refused to wear them. My mammaw was a great woman of God. She taught me about my Father in heaven, my inheritance, and all He says I am. When I say "taught," I mean preached, embedded, instilled, implanted, and ingrained.

During a period of my childhood, we all sat in the living room every Friday night, listening to the Bible on record. While my favorite television shows played in the other room, I listened to a voice, similar to James Earl Jones', slowly articulating chapter after chapter of the King James Version. It was torture. It was boring.

And it was life-changing. The Word of God, regardless of the form it reaches you, is life-changing! It is alive and breathes life into you, even when you are unaware. "For the word of God is alive and active. Sharper than any double-edged sword, it penetrates even to dividing soul and spirit, joints and marrow; it judges the thoughts and attitudes of the heart" (Heb. 4:12). God's Word pierced my soul.

As a young girl, I heard over and over, "You have a Father. He loves you. He created you. He knew you before you were born. He has a purpose for you." The Bible is not just words, written on or read from a page in a book. Those words are the actual words of God, and they speak life into whomever will hear.

And I heard I am beautiful, unique, "fearfully and wonderfully made" (Psalm 139:14). I heard my Father has a plan for me, and that plan will not harm me but will prosper me (Jer. 29:11). I heard I am forgiven and chosen, called "out of darkness into His marvelous light" (1 Peter 2:9). I am His daughter and heir. I heard all that He will do for me if I accept who I am in Him. I heard; I received; and I believed. I believed so much that I was certain if Donnie Osmond (the Justin Bieber of the seventies, for you young people) could only catch a glimpse of me, he would most certainly make me his wife.

Those words—those living, breathing words—began to drown out the voices in my head. When the voices of the enemy said I was abandoned, the Word of God said I was chosen. When they said I was ugly, the Word of God said I was altogether beautiful. When they said I was rejected, the Word of God said I was accepted. When they said I was ashamed, the Word of God said I was worthy. I believed every word of it.

From this young age, I learned to drown out the voices in my head, the lies of Satan, with the Word of my Creator, my Father, my Redeemer. I refused to wear the brands Satan tried to put on me and chose instead to wear the brands my Father wanted me to wear: brands like *beautiful, wonderfully made, loved, forgiven, adopted, accepted, powerful, worthy, courageous.* The words of the enemy are lies, but the Word of God is truth. What He says about you is who you are, but it is up to you to receive it and experience what happens in your life when you actually believe it.

When you claim your royal status and believe who God says you are, the effect is life-changing. You stop caring what other people think, comparing yourself to others, and being afraid to say yes to God when He calls. And if—well, *when*—you find your life turned upside down, perhaps even hanging from a handrail, you will have the strength to pull yourself up because you know the chaos does not define you; God simply uses it to refine you.

CROWN EFFECT 1
Stop Caring what Others Think

She said, "Let her play the witch; her teeth fit the part."

I was hurt and embarrassed; it really broke my little heart.

She said, "Meet me on the playground—I want to punch you in the face."

I stayed close to my teacher and just watched as she paced.

She said, "Look at you, it's about time you bought some new clothes."

I was shocked and bewildered but walked away, feeling low.

She said, "Your shoes are worn out," as everyone looked at my feet.

I wanted to disappear under a rock and that night cried myself to sleep.

She said, "You can't sing with the group. Your parents are divorced and in sin."

I cried like a baby and never asked again.

She said, "That's dumb, and you are just showing out."

I was looking for acceptance but instead found self-doubt.

She said, "You're having a party? I would love to come,"

Then later told my friend she knew it would be dumb.

She said, "You have to come—our girl trips are so much fun."

But when invites went out, I found I had none.

He said, "You are fearfully and wonderfully made,

"On the cross with love for you, the greatest price I paid."

I said, "I believe in Jesus, the sacrificial Lamb,

"I am a daughter of the King; my Father is the great I AM."

We all deal with mean girls who are hurtful and outspoken,

But when you know who you are, you see they're the ones broken.

In His love, grace, and mercy, I have chosen to live.

And because He forgave me, I, too, can forgive.

I WILL NEVER FORGET HER. I still see her face and hear her voice as though it were yesterday. I remember what I was wearing, where I was, and exactly how I felt that day in the eighth grade, when the bell rang for class change. I was walking down the hallway with some classmates, laughing and talking, as middle schoolers do. Mammaw had taken me shopping the day before, something we did not do often, so I had a new outfit. Right then, Miss Popularity stepped in my path, her little posse close behind. She looked me up and down with her snarly-faced expression and said, "It's about time you got some new clothes."

Everybody laughed, and I stood there, confused and stunned. What did she mean by that? Is something wrong with my clothes? At that moment, right then and there, I realized for the first time I might be poor, different. I might not fit in. Kids had said mean things that hurt my feelings before, but this time was different. She brought my own social standing into question and made me wonder what my peers thought of me. I questioned my status.

I am sure someone in your peer group has called you out before; or some jealous, hurting, broken, mean girl has tried to tear you down, doing everything she can to break you. Those mean girls (who, by the way, often grow up to be mean women) only have power over you if you give it to them. Of course, their words hurt and may send you home to cry into your pillow; but when you know who you are in Christ, the words are merely painful things that hurt your feelings and not your faith.

I did go home and cry into my pillow. I was embarrassed, and my feelings were hurt. The enemy tried to fill my head with his lying brands: *You are different. You don't fit in.* Even as an eighth grader, I was already learning who I was and that the only opinion that really matters is my heavenly Father's.

Paul speaks to the churches in Galatians 1:10 and says, "Am I now trying to win the approval of human beings, or of God? Or am I trying to please people? If I were still trying to please people, I would not be a servant of Christ." We are not to spend our lives, seeking the approval of people. Our standards or identity should not alter in order to be liked or accepted. As Paul said, we are not serving Christ if we do. That idea may sound harsh or difficult to achieve. Wanting to belong is in our very nature, but when we care more about what people think than what God thinks, we serve them, not Him.

The Bible tells a beautiful story about a woman who washed Jesus' feet with perfume from an alabaster jar (Luke 7:36-50). Her name is not given, but she was known as a sinner in her community, a harlot. We can learn many lessons from this story, but one thing that stands out is how she was impervious to the possible reactions of others in the room. This woman was inside the house of a Pharisee, known for strict adherence to the law, but did not allow her fear of what he would think, say, or do interfere with this opportunity to serve her King. She walked right up to Jesus, weeping, and poured her expensive perfume on His feet.

What did Jesus do? He defended her and reproved the Pharisee. What a great moment that must have been for this woman, who most assuredly had been mocked and ridiculed for her sinful life! She walked away that day, knowing who she was in Christ, how much He loved her, and that her life would never be the same! We all want to fit in and be accepted; but when you start believing who God says you are, you stop valuing man's opinion over God's approval.

We circle back to Miss Popularity. While her opinion of me and my clothing did not matter, her ambush was still embarrassing. She and her posse appeared like a pride of lions about to pounce on a gazelle and went straight for the kill. Her words cut deeply, like the claws of a lion's paw, but what hurt the most was the laughter. My peers and even some of my friends laughed at me. Most middle school kids will follow the class bully, simply to avoid becoming the target of her aggression. Although all she did was roar, she did lead the pride. I had a decision to make. Would I allow her words to control me? Would I give her power over how I felt about myself and treated others? Would I join her pride and become someone I did not want to be, or would I follow the Lion of the tribe of Judah, the all-powerful King of kings, Who not only roars but conquers?

In Acts 5, Peter and the apostles were arrested and put in jail by a jealous high priest and his associates. During the night, though, an angel of the Lord opened the doors of the jail to release them. The angel ordered them to go stand in the temple courts and tell the people all about this new life. They did and were, once again, taken by soldiers to face the high priest, who asked why they defied his orders. They replied, "'We must obey God rather than human beings!'" (Acts 5:29).

You also have a decision to make. Who will be the ruler of your life and lead you to become the person you were created to be? Will you listen to people and the roar of the enemy or the words of your Father? When you truly believe who God says you are, you realize that the person trying to tear you down is usually the one who needs to look upward. You will always have an adversary—someone who, for whatever reason, gets under your skin and makes you feel unworthy. Will you spend your time, pursuing validation from someone who does not like who you are, or will you seek the approval of the One Who created you and loves the real you? God's opinion is what matters; under His authority, you will not only know who you are, but you will also become all He created you to be.

CROWN EFFECT 2
Stop Comparing Yourself to Others

WE ALL DO IT. WE see a woman who has what we desire and think, *Why not me?* Maybe you look at her engagement ring, her baby bump, her girl trip pictures, or her house and think, *Why can I not have those things?* You notice her social media likes and perfectly toned body; you witness her talent, education, or career. You watch her flawless life unfold and think, *Why can that not be me?*

If we are honest with ourselves, we all know her life is not perfect! We live in a fallen world. All of our lives are huge messes, filled with chaos and dysfunction at some level. Remember me? I am still flashing the congregation! Sadly, social media enables people to selectively and artistically present what appears to be a perfect life; if you are not careful, you will start comparing your mess to their masterpieces.

The reality is that hurt and sadness can lurk behind any perfect smile. Any idyllic family vacation can be marred by a family fight. With every impeccably decorated home comes bills, broken appliances, dirty laundry, unidentifiable smells, and possibly the occasional mouse that found its way to that six-month-old Christmas candy in the nightstand drawer—not that this ever happened to me, of course! Behind any aesthetically enviable social media masterpiece, you could find a mess! Because of grace, though, behind every child of God is a work in progress: a beautiful soul, sitting on the Potter's wheel, being molded into who she was created to be. That child of God is a mess, being made into a masterpiece by the One Who formed her in the womb and knew her before she was born.

Comparison is the enemy's way of keeping you from seeing who God created you to be. Satan wants you to feel unworthy, insecure, and incapable. What better way than to have you look at another woman's social media masterpiece and think that God must love her more or that she must be a better person? It is easy to think that life is not fair or that you got the short end of the stick, but remember that Satan is "a liar and the father of lies" (John 8:44). When you compare yourself with others, you agree with his lies.

One day, not too long ago, I was sitting by myself on the beach and happened to notice my five-dollar flip flops, lying in the sand. They looked pretty worn out, and I decided I need a new pair. Right then, the Lord spoke to my heart. "If you could walk in any woman's flip flops, whose would they be?" Was it a trick question? Should I answer with someone like Mary, the mother of Jesus, or Esther, who saved her entire nation from annihilation? I pondered and then answered honestly and emphatically. "No one's!" I cannot think of another woman whose flip flops I want to walk in.

That question brought an amazing realization to my life. Yes, I can think of many smarter, prettier, more talented women who accomplish more, have more, and do more. I respect and learn from several women, none of whom fall and flash everyone in church! But I would not want to walk in any of their flip flops because I know *this* woman. I know where her flip flops have been and can recount all the marvelous things her Father has done for her. I know where her flips flops are now and the peace she has in knowing her Father has a great plan for her. Although I do not know exactly where she is going, I know her Father has paved the way and is going with her. For those reasons, I am completely satisfied, walking in my own five-dollar flip flops—or my pink rhinestone flip flops, pink cork-heeled platform shoes, pink western-style ankle boots, or—my favorite—pink leather and suede, fur-lined duck boots.

Whether you walk in flip flops, combat boots, sneakers, or stilettos, never wish you could walk in another woman's shoes. Yours are a perfect fit; and if the shoes fit, walk in them! Walk in your own shoes, knowing you are "fearfully and wonderfully made" (Psalm 139:14) from the top of your head to the soles of your feet. Trust God to take you places you never dreamed you could go. Walk in your own shoes, believing that He will be there to pick you up, even if you stumble and fall.

And know these three things:

1. Your Father does not love her more than He loves you. His love for us is so great that we cannot begin to understand it. As humans, our love for one another usually depends on the behavior of the person we love or are trying to love. Boundaries, qualifications, and exceptions do not limit God's love. It is so "wide and long and high and deep" that it "surpasses knowledge" (Eph. 3:18-19). He

loves you just as you are, and you can do nothing to change it. The Bible tells us that nothing in all creation can separate us from the love of God—nothing you have said, no mistake you have made, and no mess you find yourself in will take away His love for you. It is infinite, unfailing, and unconditional.

2. Your Father is not rewarding her for being a better person. We are saved by grace, which is a gift from God. No amount of work or good can earn His grace; you need only ask. James 4 teaches us to humble ourselves and draw near to God. It is then that He will lift and hold us up. Stop looking at Debbie Do-it-all, poster child for church and volunteer work. She is doing what God called her to do, using her gifts to serve Him, which is wonderful. A person can preach, teach, serve, and give; but not one word, lesson, meal, nor dollar will earn His grace. It is free to all who simply call on Him.

3. She did not win the blessings lottery. Life is not always fair, and everyone is not on the same playing field. Look at my life. It certainly did not start on a level playing field, but that was actually the best thing to ever happen to me. Yes, I was abandoned as a young child, but that abandonment led me to a place where I was loved unconditionally and taught about the unconditional love of Jesus. It led me to salvation and learning who I am in Christ and to living an abundant life. Getting the short end of the stick may be how God prepares you for all He has in store for you. Trust Him and know He is in control.

While you look around, comparing yourself, desiring someone else's life, you miss out on the life God has planned for you. Romans 12:2 says, "Do not conform to the pattern of this world, but be transformed by the renewing of your mind. Then you will be able to test and approve what God's will is—his good, pleasing and perfect will." Transformation starts with your thinking and focus. Spend your days reading the Word and listening to what God says to you, instead of thinking about what God does for someone else. Focus on submitting yourself completely to Him, just as you are, and allowing Him to mold you into who you were created to be. Then you will discover how wonderful it is to live in the center of His will for you, rather than sitting on the sidelines of His will for someone else.

Now, am I saying you will never look at another woman and wish you had what she does? No way! But when you know who you are in Him and you believe who you are in Him, you will know what He has for you is so much more! Although you may wish for what she has, you will not look at her and think, *Why not me?* See her, remembering that all you want to be is yourself—even if your self is clinging to a handrail, thinking how different things might be if you had worn those five-dollar flip flops to church!

CROWN EFFECT 3
Stop Being Afraid to Say Yes to God

HAVE YOU READ THE BIBLICAL story of Esther? Talk about chaos!

Esther was an orphan, being raised by an uncle and living in exile. The Bible does not go into detail, but this young girl's life was turned upside down at some point. She lost both parents and had to go live with another family member. I can speak from experience as to how traumatic this situation can be. I can see Esther, daydreaming of what life would be like if her parents were still with her, thinking of her future, and praying something would fill the holes in her heart, never imagining she would catch the eye of a king.

And then it happens. The king not only notices her, but he also chooses her. She goes from orphan in exile to beloved queen of Persia. Like you and me, though, Esther lived in a fallen world, so chaos did not end there. Her uncle, Mordecai, refused to bow to the king's adviser Haman, making him angry enough to want all Jewish people killed. Haman convinced the king to "destroy, kill and annihilate all the Jews" (Esther 3:13).

Mordecai sent word to Esther about the law, convincing her to approach King Xerxes—who adored her but did not know she was Jewish—and plead for mercy for her people, even though she knew that going before the king meant she could be put to death.

> [Mordecai] sent back this answer: "Do not think that because you are in the king's house you alone of all the Jews will escape. For if you remain silent at this time, relief and deliverance for the Jews will arise from another place, but you and your father's family will perish. And who knows but that you have come to your royal position for such a time as this?" Then Esther sent this reply to Mordecai: "Go, gather all the Jews who are in Susa, and fast for me. Do not eat or drink for three days, night or day. I and my attendants will fast as you do. When this is done, I will go to the king, even though it is against the law. And if I perish, I perish" (Esther 4:13-16).

She went to the king, found favor with him once again, and saved the Jewish people. The story of Esther sounds like a fairy tale. A poor, unknown young girl becomes a beautiful, beloved queen. But Esther is not a character in a storybook; she was a real woman, and her story was planned and written by God for a purpose—"for such a time as this."

Just like Esther, God has a plan and purpose for you. It was not coincidence that Esther became queen. God knew she had the courage to do whatever it took to save her people. Do you have that kind of courage? Can God count on you to do His calling? Will you use the abilities, resources, connections, and opportunities He has given you to fulfill your purpose "for such a time as this"? If you truly believe who God says you are, the answer to all these questions will be, "Yes, God! Yes!"

I was an educator at the same school for thirty-two years. For the last nine, I was the principal. I loved my job, the school, the community, staff, and students. No matter how hard it was at times, I never thought I would be able to leave, certain they would have to drag me out, kicking and screaming, one day. Then something felt different. God had a plan, and I decided to retire. No one was more surprised than I was. Many people speculated about why I left. Rumors circulated. Some people were mad. The truth is, I was not sure why I left. I knew only that God was calling.

Now, He was not calling me to a purpose as big as Esther's. I have certainly not had to risk my life, but I did have to jump—to decide to leave something I loved so deeply and take a risk "for such a time as this." I had to be courageous! In His time, God revealed His plan: He was calling me to write this book! Truthfully, He had already placed it on my heart; I had tried, but it was impossible with so many demands in my life. I simply did not have the time, so my Father put things in motion to provide the time. I had to say yes!

Terrified? Yes! Worried? Yes! Uncertain? Yes! Unworthy? Yes! Incapable? Yes! How could I do this? I had been an educator since I was twenty-four years old. I did not know how to be anything else, and I did not want to be. But this book was on my heart, and God confirmed time and again that I had not completely lost my mind. He was calling, so I found the courage to say yes to God; and His plan for me was fulfilled. I know this to be true because you are reading my book, and oh, how I pray it makes a difference in your life!

In Ephesians 1:11, Paul said, "In him we were also chosen, having been predestined according to the plan of him who works out everything in conformity with the purpose of his will." God has a purpose for you. You are chosen and predestined to walk in that purpose; but when the time comes, you must be able to hear Him and be willing to say yes. You may be thinking, *How do I hear Him?* Well, for Esther, it was easy. Her uncle plainly told her what she should do and the consequences if she refused. No one approached me to say, "Hey, you need to retire and write a book." God did plant the seeds in my heart and created a chain of events that led me straight to my employer's human resources office.

Psalm 32:8 says, "I will instruct you and teach you in the way you should go; I will counsel you with my loving eye on you." If you want to hear from God, spend time with Him. Read His Word. Be still and listen. He will teach you, lead you, and show you the way. He will let you know when it is your time. Remember that "'everything is possible for one who believes'" (Mark 9:23). With Him you can do anything (Phil. 4:13)! With Him you can find the courage to say yes.

As I am still over here, hanging upside down, maybe—just maybe—I can find the courage to pull myself up (and my dress down) and say yes to the nice man at the end of the row, who keeps asking if I am okay!

Pause for Reflection

"When he [the devil] lies, he speaks his native language,
for he is a liar and the father of lies."

John 8:44

What lies do you hear from the enemy? List any of his brands you currently wear: _____

_____

_____

What does the Bible say about who you are? Write five things God says about you: _____

_____

_____

_____

Why is it sometimes easier to believe Satan's lies over God's truth? __

_____

_____

_____

"Finally, brothers and sisters, whatever is true, whatever is noble, whatever is right, whatever is pure, whatever is lovely, whatever is admirable—if anything is excellent or praiseworthy—think about such things."

Philippians 4:8

Do the enemy's lies fit into this Scripture as something you should think about? Write some things you should dwell on instead. _____

_____

_____

_____

_____

Have you allowed someone else's opinion make you feel unworthy or insignificant? Why do her thoughts matter to you? _____

_____

_____

_____

_____

In Galatians 1:10, Paul says, "If I were still trying to please people, I would not be a servant of Christ."

How does caring about what other people think keep you from serving Christ? _____

_____

_____

_____

_____

Do you sometimes compare your messy life to someone else's social media masterpiece? While you dwell on what God is doing in her life, what happens to the plans God has for you? _____

_____

_____

_____

_____

_____

_____

Have you been afraid to say yes to God in the past or present? What holds you back? _____

_____

_____

_____

_____

_____

_____

List four things you can do to hear from God and find the courage to say yes. _____

_____

_____

_____

_____

_____

_____

Romans 12:2 says to "be transformed by the renewing of your mind."

What does this instruction mean? _____

_____

_____

_____

_____

What steps can you take to renew your mind and be transformed? __

_____

_____

_____

_____

CHAPTER 2
Love Yourself

I RECENTLY HAD A FIGHT—AN all-out, wrestle-on-the-floor, sweaty, red-faced fight! It is crazy, I know; but those white jeans just would not give, and I had had all I could take! I will not mention who won the fight, but I will tell you that scissors were involved. Does that scenario sound familiar? How often do you find yourself in an all-out battle over how you look or, rather, how you see yourself? How often are you unhappy with your body, abilities, talents, or personality traits? And how often does this battle begin simply because of what they say?

Who are *they*, you ask? Well, that depends. Who has your attention? Whose opinion do you value? Who do you want to look like, act like, be like? Whoever that answer is usually sets the criteria for your battlefields. You desire to look like, accomplish as, even be who they say you should. When you do not feel you measure up, you fight a poor self-image that leads to insecurities and possibly even anxiety or depression—all because of what *they* say.

I would love to tell you how easy it is to stop caring what they say about you, but I cannot. Look at Eve in Genesis 3:1-7. She lived in paradise but still listened to what they said. In this case, *they* was the devil himself! With all God provided, Eve wanted more and believed Satan's suggestion that she would be like God if she only ate the fruit. We all know how that unfolded!

On the other hand, consider women in the Bible who refused to listen to what they say. Remember Sarah—childless at the age of ninety and, no doubt, in menopause? I am certain most people said she would never give Abraham a child. But Sarah did not listen to what they said; she believed God and not only bore a son but became the "mother of nations" (Gen. 17:16). Rahab, a woman with a bad reputation, did not listen to what her own people said about God, recognizing His greatness from stories she heard (Josh. 2). Choosing to ignore what they said and to follow Him, she helped the Israeli spies, who, in turn, spared her life. She became part of the lineage of Jesus Christ.

When Ruth lost her husband, family and friends encouraged her to go back home, claiming she had no obligation to stay with her mother-in-law. Ruth did not listen to what they said (Ruth 1). She was a woman of character and integrity and cared more about doing right than what others thought was best for her. She believed God is Who He says He is. She believed He would provide, and He did.

Can you imagine what people said about Mary and probably directly to her? Can you just hear all the advice this young girl was given? She listened to the angel of the Lord instead of what they said and went on to birth our Savior (Matt. 1:18-25).

How people must have talked about a woman in leadership during Old Testament times! But prophetess and judge Deborah was faithful and obedient, listening only to God (Judges 4-5). Trusting in His power, she delivered the Israelites from bondage.

Let us not forget Esther, the queen. Surely, everyone around her warned that if she went to the king on behalf of the Jews, she would surely die. Why would an orphan girl-turned-queen take a chance on losing everything? She chose not to listen to what they said, obeying God's plan instead, and an entire nation was rescued (Esther 5-10).

All these plain, simple, ordinary women, likely confused about their places in the world, chose to listen to God and were used for His glory. If what they say does not align with the Word of God, it is a lie. We must know, believe, and walk in the truth; and the truth is that God does not see you the way man sees. Just as He did not see Sarah as barren, Rahab as unclean, Deborah as ambitious, Ruth as hopeless, Esther as weak, or Mary as a mere child, He does not see you as they say you are. He sees your heart (I Sam. 16:7).

In Acts 13:22, Paul says, "After removing Saul, he made David their king. God testified concerning him: 'I have found David son of Jesse, a man after my own heart; he will do everything I want him to do.'" This one statement tells us everything we need to know about what God saw in David and what we should strive to see in ourselves.

1. God said He "found" David, which means He was looking. God is looking for servants to do His will, not bend to the will of the world.

2. God said David was "a man after my own heart," which means he pleased God. God wants us to seek Him and humble ourselves before Him, not seek the acceptance and admiration of the world around us.

3. God said, "He will do everything I want him to do,"
    which means David had a desire to obey God. He was
    willing to not only do what God wanted him to do but
    also to complete the will of God without compromise.

When God looked at David, He saw his heart. He saw someone willing, eager, and obedient; He saw someone who would not compromise the will of God to please others or get what he wanted. God saw potential.

In order to love yourself, you must start by seeing yourself the way God sees you. God looks for potential, not perfection. He does not see your extra weight; He sees how you carry the weight of a burden for people in need. He does not see your chipped nail polish; He sees hands that feed the hungry, reach out to the brokenhearted, and work tirelessly to provide and make a home for your family. He does not see your big shoe size but feet that run after Him, seeking His face and longing for more of Him. He does not see the color of your hair, eyes, skin; He looks at how you color the world with love and kindness, compassion and understanding, grace and mercy.

He does not see your brokenness but rather how He can use your experiences to help others as a testament of what He can do. Instead of your guilt and shame, He sees that your sins are forgiven through Christ and how you offer forgiveness to others. He does not see your rejection but that you belong to Him; He sees how you include people who often feel excluded. He does not see your loneliness because He is with you wherever you go. He does not see your granny panties; He sees your ability to overcome even the most humiliating circumstances. He does not see your flaws. He sees your potential.

That fight I had with my jeans was not about my need to lose weight or buy a larger size. It was about seeing myself through the eyes of the world. It was about believing a lie while ignoring the truth, seeking perfection in the world instead of potential in Him. For centuries, women have tried to live up to a standard of perfection that simply cannot be achieved—a standard based on what they say instead of what God sees. When you see yourself through the eyes of the world, you allow the enemy to steal your opportunities, interfere with your purpose, and stand in the way of your potential. When you see yourself as your Creator does, you strive to be healthy, in order to do all He wants. You work harder to be who He wants you to be, rising above your insecurities to go wherever He wants. When you love yourself, you stop standing behind closed doors. You shake off whatever holds you back and prosper, knowing your worth cannot be measured by anything *they say*.

Now, I can well imagine what they are saying about me—a middle-aged woman who was late for church, fell, and continues to dangle there, wondering how (after showing her underpants) she can ever show her face again.

CROWN EFFECT 4
Stop Standing Behind Closed Doors

OKAY, THIS ONE MAY HURT a bit, but may I be honest? Sometimes, you just have to get over it and move on with life. For many reasons, you do not always get what you want. The reality is that some doors close, leaving you with a life-changing decision. Will you stand behind that door, feeling inadequate, unworthy, and rejected; allowing the enemy to brand you a failure; spending all your time and energy, trying to pry the door open? Or will you accept that maybe the door is closed for a reason and move on with your life? Maybe you were not the most qualified for that job; or you were, and nepotism got in the way. Maybe you were the problem in the relationship, or that person was not who you thought. Maybe your talent is not as good as you think, or somebody else was just better. Maybe you made a mistake, or it just was not the right time. Maybe it is just life, and no blame exists.

Maybe God closed the door. It may have nothing to do with your qualifications, problems, talents, mistakes, how much you deserve it, nor how well you did. It may simply be an act of God. Maybe He is trying to rescue you, deliver you, work on you, or simply take you to the next level; yet here you stand, behind this closed door, refusing to move.

Many people love Jeremiah 29:11: "'For I know the plans I have for you,' declares the LORD, 'plans to prosper you and not to harm you, plans to give you hope and a future.'" We write it in high school yearbooks, print it on our children's graduation announcements, and even tattoo it on our bodies. We often overlook the most important part of this verse. God said, "*I* know the plans *I* have for you." His plans may not include the ideas we have for ourselves. Surrendering every facet of life to Him is one of the hardest things a follower of Christ will do. If you want to see God's purpose fulfilled in your life, if you want to walk in His perfect will, then you must trust that He knows what is best. Sometimes what is best leaves you standing behind a closed door.

No one likes closed doors. You want what you want; when you do not get it, you are disappointed and want to know why. The truth is that God's plans for you may not include getting everything you want. If you wait on Him, He will show you His way; however, His way cannot be found while standing behind a closed door. The worst experience I ever had with a closed door was when my son, my lastborn, walked out our front door for the last time as a single man. The wedding was beautiful; and I gained a daughter-in-law, who is everything I prayed she would be. But I was left standing behind that closed door, wondering for the first time in twenty-seven years who I was and what I was going to do with my life.

It is funny how life brings so many things for which we cannot prepare. I was unprepared for the overwhelming love I felt for my children in the moments they were born or for going the next two years without a complete night's sleep. I did not anticipate the fear that came every time they were sick, fell down, or simply left my sight. Many first-time experiences brought me great joy and some introduced overwhelming fear and anguish. Needless to say, nothing prepared me for motherhood. But I had done it. I had raised two amazing children who love the Lord, have great jobs, and are homeowners. They are everything I prayed they would be, and I could not be prouder.

The problem was that they are everything I prayed they would be: happy, independent adults who left the nest to build their own lives . . . without me. We will always be close and spend time together, but they will never live in my house again. That door closed; and trust me, nothing prepared me for it. I was heartbroken and lost. For a while, I just stood behind that door, knowing it would not open but unable to move. You would think I would have remembered that God's grace is sufficient for any major changes in life, but obviously, I did not. I cried on my children's first days of elementary school, middle school, and high school; when they went on their first dates; when they became licensed to drive. I cried when I moved them into the college dormitories and into their first homes.

Life comes in seasons, and each season must come to an end. At every end, I cried and wondered if I would ever be happy again. But with each ending came a new beginning, and it was not long before I realized that God was not finished with me yet. Consequently, in each season, He was teaching and preparing me for the next. God's plans for me did not end when my son walked out and closed that door; rather, He was just getting started. His plans give us hope and a future. He still had so much planned for me, but I had to be willing to move.

A closed door may leave you heartbroken and tearful; but it should never leave you insecure, and it certainly should not steal your confidence. Hebrews 10:35-36 says, "So do not throw away your confidence; it will be richly rewarded. You need to persevere so that when you have done the will of God, you will receive what he has promised." We all want to be richly rewarded and receive what God has promised, so we must remain confident and persevere in all circumstances. Perseverance is not standing behind a closed door, crying, blaming yourself or others, feeling rejected, struggling to pry the door back open. No, perseverance is confidently seeking and doing the will of God. Rest assured, you will not find His will while standing behind a door that will not open.

When God closes a door of opportunity, it cannot be reopened. When He opens a door, it can never be closed. Remain confident. Persevere. Seek His will. Look for the open doors. See yourself the way God sees you. He has so much planned for you in this and every season of your life. You just have to be willing to move on—a piece of advice I probably need to heed myself as I cling to this handrail, contemplating my next move.

CROWN EFFECT 5
Shake Off What Holds You Back

ONE OF MY ALL-TIME FAVORITE movies is *The Parent Trap*. In one scene, the twins are stuck on a camping trip with their future step-monster. Obviously in excellent physical shape, she mysteriously struggles on the hike because the girls are gradually filling her backpack with rocks. As you can imagine, over time, the excess weight of what she carries begins to hinder her progress and her ability to get where she is going. I think we can all relate to this in some way.

Maybe you picked up some rocks along the path of your life—bad decisions that pulled you away from the will of God, negative people who pushed you down, excuses that keep you from moving forward, or a negative attitude that separates you from the purpose God has planned for your life—all of which hold you back and hinder your forward progress. You may not even realize you carry this extra weight, but ask yourself, *Do I keep making the same mistakes, knowing I am not obeying God? Am I burdened or depressed, unable to find the strength for what I want or need to do? Do I always find an excuse for not doing what I feel called to do? Do I allow negative people to affect how*

I feel about myself? If so, you may need to shake off some things that weigh you down and hold you back.

Life is hard. Bad things happen. Sometimes, the bad things result from bad choices. You make decisions every day that influence your future and relationship with God. Every decision that does not align with the Word of God adds rocks to your backpack. You carry the weight of guilt or regret or are burdened with the consequences of actions that not only affect you but also the people you love. You start to feel unworthy of God's promises. Sin opens the door for the enemy, who loves nothing more than to have a reason to whisper his lies in your ear.

Know that Christ came to free you from sin. He forgives, and you get to start over with a clean slate. Stop repeating the same cycle because you feel you cannot be forgiven. You can! Maybe you did bring it upon yourself; the consequences are hard; and the devil is beating you up about it. Consider the words of John 3:17: "For God did not send his Son into the world to condemn the world, but to save the world through him." You do not have to carry the weight of condemnation. Jesus died, so you can be free from the burden of sin. Shake off your mistakes or bad decisions. And while you let go of guilt and regret, you may need to let go of some people in your life.

Jesus called us to love all people, but, as Paul reminds us in 1 Corinthians 15:33, "Bad company corrupts good character." So, while you must love everyone, you do not have to keep company with all of them! You know who I mean. You probably thought of them immediately—the friend who is not a positive influence;

the one who walked away and left you hurt and wondering why; the one who has never been a friend, but you want so badly to be in her circle; the ex who walked out; the family member who drains your bank account and your sanity; the coworker who is determined to undermine you; the hater who does not want to see you succeed. They may not be bad people; they may just be bad for you. If they hold you back, it is time to let them go. Decide to move on from people who drag you down. Quit blaming yourself for lost relationships, trying to figure out what went wrong and why they no longer accept you. Stop allowing them to steal your peace of mind. Love them but let them go.

While you let go of these people, it may also be time to let go of the negative effect their words have on you. Words are powerful. The Bible says the tongue holds the power of life and death (Prov. 18:21). For whatever reason, some people spew negativity like ash from a volcano, leaving their victims scarred by the powerful heaviness of their insults, taunts, or snide remarks. While their comments may have been delivered under the pretense of a joke, if you are the target, you may carry the weight of those negative words. You may start to believe the put-downs, doubt yourself, and worry about what people think of you. The weight of those words may keep you from walking in your purpose.

If you have the power to simply shake off that ash and move on, then good for you. If it starts weighing you down, though, it may be time to shake off the person who spews the ash. Do not allow negative words to keep you from seeing yourself the way God does. He sees your potential, not your perfection. I know how hard it can be to let go. My goodness, I have a hard time letting go of anything! I have a closet filled with clothes that have long gone out of style, a storage room of home décor I know I will never use again, and an entire storage building filled with a lifetime of stuff stacked high. My excuse for keeping it is that I may use it again someday. You know what? None of that accumulation holds me back. I do not carry it around like rocks in a backpack, and I do not allow it to keep me from moving forward. So, I will keep making excuses and adding to the pile!

However, the regret of bad decisions, influence of negative people, and sting of negative words weighs you down; and no good excuse exists for holding on to them. How many times have you said, "I want to move on, but . . ." or "I would let go if . . ."? Stop making excuses. Those ifs and buts only keep you from freeing yourself of your burden. Empty your backpack of everything that weighs you down and make a commitment to pack light as you move forward on your journey through life.

Now, I must admit that packing light is just not an option when I travel. No matter how much my luggage weighs, how much the airline charges, how much room I have—I cannot do it. I would rather hold my suitcase in my lap than not have what I need—or, at least, what I think I need! I look at my luggage and know I will never touch most of what is inside. It is heavy and will probably be a burden to me. Carrying it will probably hold me back, but I still cannot find one thing I am willing to leave behind, so I take it all with me. Is that not what we do when we carry the weight of regret, disappointment, pain, and guilt?

It is time to lighten your load. Stop carrying regret—you are forgiven. Let go of people who hurt, rejected, or had a bad influence on you—you are loved. Let go of negative words that made you feel unworthy of the blessings of God—you are chosen. Stop the excuses—you are strong. I challenge you to leave behind anything you do not need and anything that burdens you or holds you back. Put simply, I challenge you to forgive, let go, get over it, and cut yourself some slack!

If someone hurt you, forgive her because your Savior forgave you. The Bible says, "For all have sinned and fall short of the glory of God" (Rom. 3:23). It is easy to quote this Scripture, but we tend to overlook the *all* in the verse. We "*all* have sinned." We "*all* fall short of the glory of God," but because God sent His Son to shed His blood and die on the cross, we all can be forgiven. If your heavenly Father can forgive you, who are you to withhold forgiveness? Despite the circumstance, pain, or excuses, if you want to be forgiven, you must forgive. If you want to pack lightly, forgive people who hurt you. Do not carry the pain around with you.

If you made mistakes, let go of regret. You cannot carry the regret of those mistakes with you forever. If you wronged or hurt someone, ask forgiveness and do what you can to fix it. Other than that, you have to move on—it is okay to let go of the burden of regretting what could have or should have been. If you think about it, how ridiculous it is to carry that load when you can do absolutely nothing about it. You cannot change the past. Let go and let yourself move forward, having learned something that will make the future even better. Do not take the burden of regret with you!

If you did not get what you wanted or failed to reach your goals, get over it. So what—you did not lose the weight last year; you did not get that degree, job, promotion. Maybe your life does not look like you thought it would by now, and you are disappointed. If you carry that disappointment around with you like a fully-packed piece of Horizon 70 Louis Vuitton luggage (a girl can dream, can she not?), you will find yourself with something valuable that can never reach its destination. You cannot move forward if you focus on what you did not achieve, instead of working toward what you wish to achieve. You cannot move forward carrying the weight of disappointment.

If you have done all you can do, cut yourself some slack. Oh, how our society has a way of making women feel guilty! We are too nice, or we are too assertive. We are too emotional or too detached, too weak or too aggressive, too passive or too driven, too generous or too selfish. We are too skinny, or we are too fat (oh yes, I went there!). You can rarely have a conversation with a woman about the past without her saying, "I wish I had . . . " You wish you had what—been perfect; made all the right decisions; been everything for everybody, all day, every day? You know better than to think that is possible. You know you should not feel guilty, so cut yourself some slack, let go of the guilt, and move on. Guilt serves only to keep you from being who God created you to be and to keep you from fulfilling His purpose in you. Who cares what society says? You know what God says.

It makes me so sad to see women burdened with the weight of hurt, regret, disappointment, and guilt. It makes me so mad that Satan uses these things to try to steal, kill, and destroy you. But you can do something about it: believe it when God says, "'Forget the former things; do not dwell on the past. See, I am doing a new thing! Now it springs up; do you not perceive it? I am making a way in the wilderness and streams in the wasteland'" (Isa. 43:18-19).

Your Father says not to dwell on the past. Obey Him. Start packing light and see what you can do! Start packing light and see what *God* will do!

CROWN EFFECT 6

Prosper, Knowing Your Worth Cannot Be Measured

I REMEMBER WATCHING THE ANNUAL beauty pageant in my high school auditorium, imagining what it would be like to participate—to shop for the perfect dress, have my hair and makeup done professionally, walk out on that stage with confidence, and be crowned the most beautiful girl in school. Then I woke up. The truth was that my hair was always cut and permed at home, I would not know where to shop for a dress, and, at that age, poise and elegance were not my friends—so, no, I never had the opportunity to wear that much-coveted pageant crown.

I did not fully realize it at the time, but I already owned the most beautiful crown that carries the most important title any girl could want, and I did not have to compete for it. I had no need to covet a pageant crown when I had access to my own, bought and paid for by my Father, the King.

Sister, you must never forget Who your Father is. You are royal, created for greatness, uniquely fashioned, valuable, and worthy of all God has planned for you. You may not always feel worthy, and you certainly do not always feel royal. Sometimes, you probably feel more like a pauper than a princess.

You may be a young woman, dealing with bullying and low self-esteem. You may be a new mommy, up to your ears in dirty diapers, nasal syringes, and projectile vomit; or perhaps you dream of having children but have not been able to conceive. Maybe you face midlife with a husband and teenagers, hot flashes, weight gain, and more demands on your time than you feel you can handle; or you are an empty-nester, lonely and confused, wondering what to do with your life now that it no longer revolves around someone else. You may be grieving a loved one, doubting you will ever be happy again. A seasoned woman, perhaps you worry about health issues and fear what the future holds. Or you may just be trying to get by, dealing with loneliness, chaos, sickness, heartbreak, or stress. No matter who you are, how you feel, or what you face, if you know Jesus as your Savior, your heritage remains the same. You are a daughter of the King, and your birthright comes with a crown.

It is not about your circumstances. How you feel, where you have been, and what you have done are irrelevant. Your popularity and what you have to offer are insignificant. It is about whether you choose to see yourself the way God sees you and value yourself the way you are valued by God. How valuable are you to God? Well, how valuable are your children to you?

Remember how excited you were, preparing for the big arrival? Can you recall that incredible, unbelievable feeling that overwhelmed you when you first held your son or daughter? It is love like no other and a feeling that never leaves, even when they grow up and move away from home. You will protect them at any cost; fight for them anywhere, anytime, anyhow; love them, regardless of what they say or do. They mean more to you than anything else on this earth and are more valuable to you than anything you will ever possess. That is how much your Father in Heaven values you.

God created you. David says it best in Psalm 139. God formed your inward parts and "knit [you] together in [your] mother's womb" (v. 13). Your days were planned before you were even born. Jesus says you are more valuable to Him than the birds of the air and the flowers of the field. As a child of God, you are "precious and honored in his sight" (Isa. 43:4).

When Jesus was on earth, He showed nothing but love and compassion for mankind, healing the sick, feeding the hungry, defending the children, and extending grace to the sinner. He even forgave the people who crucified Him. No greater love exists than the love He has for you. God paid a price for you. He allowed His Son Jesus to die on the cross to pay for your sin. He paid that high price because He loves His creation and wants to be in communion with you. He wants a relationship with you now and for eternity. He wants to save, redeem, bless, pour His grace on you, and use you for His purpose.

A thief hung on the cross that was next to Jesus. In all His pain and suffering, at the point of death, Jesus extended him grace. While he neither earned nor deserved it, he received it because Jesus loved him. God has invested in you. From the moment you were conceived, He saw your potential and began a work in you that was planned and prepared before you were even born. You are "God's special possession, [chosen to] declare the praises of him who called you out of darkness into his marvelous light" (1 Peter 2:9).

You are God's handiwork—the result of His creation, salvation, redemption, restoration, and sanctification. Physical beauty, poise, elegance, financial status, education, or anything of this world have no bearing on your value. It is not increased by any title you hold. Your true worth cannot be measured. God created you, paid a high price for you, and has invested in you. It is up to you to make certain His investment pays off. You can spend your life, longing for the things of this world and measuring yourself by its ideals, or you can believe your value is so high it cannot be measured by worldly standards. You can believe what God says about you and love yourself just as the person He created you to be.

Pause For Reflection

Reflect for a moment on how you see yourself. Does that perspective sometimes mirror what people say instead of what God says? _____

_____

_____

Why do you think Eve listened to the lies of Satan? _____

_____

_____

Why do you think Sarah, Rahab, Deborah, Ruth, Esther, and Mary listened to and believed God? _____

_____

_____

Acts 13:22 notes that God saw David as a *"man after my own heart."*

What does God see when He looks at you? _____

_____

_____

Does He see a woman who will obey Him without compromising to meet the world's expectations? Does He see a woman who seeks to please Him or longs to be accepted by the people around her? _____

_____

_____

_____

Have you ever tried to open a door that has been closed to you? Describe the circumstances and discuss how you might handle a closed-door situation differently in the future. _____

_____

_____

_____

_____

What steps can you take to fully surrender your will to obey God and accept what He has for you? _____

_____

_____

_____

_____

Have you picked up rocks throughout life that continue to weigh you down? List them below.

Regrets: _____

_____

_____

People: _____

_____

_____

Negative words: _____

_____

_____

Failures: _____

_____

_____

Disappointments: _____

_____

_____

Guilt: _____

_____

_____

"Forget the former things; do not dwell in the past."

Isaiah 43:18

Those rocks in your backpack cause you to dwell in the past. What steps can you take to lighten your load? _____

_____

_____

Do you sometimes measure yourself by your physical beauty, financial status, education, or talent? David says in Psalm 139 that you are "fearfully and wonderfully made." What does this idea mean? _____

_____

_____

_____

_____

_____

Do you see yourself as a daughter of the King of kings, a princess with an inheritance? As a child of God, that is who you are. _____

_____

_____

_____

_____

_____

CHAPTER 3

Walk in His Light

I AM STILL OVER HERE, gripping the handrail! The fall should not have surprised me, but it did. Why was I not more careful? How could I have prevented it? And why, in all that is merciful and holy, did God allow me to lose my footing? He might have rendered me unconscious, so I could be carried away—a faceless pair of granny panties, who just might be able to show her face at church again.

But the truth is that I know the answer—it was dark. I was late; the lights were dimmed; and I now understand what older people mean when they claim not to see well at night. I missed that step because I did not see it. The darkness caused my fall—not me and certainly not God.

When we walk in darkness, we cannot see where we are going; we cannot see obstacles in our way; and we cannot see danger. Unfortunately, we live in a dark world, where we may stumble, lose momentum, or get stuck at any time. We may find ourselves falling backward.

One minute, you are advancing in your career with opportunities for more responsibility and higher pay; the next, you are starting over.

You are paying all the bills on time; and suddenly, you have more month than money. You may be well on your way to goal weight and then find yourself eating a quart of emotional-support ice cream. Your house is in order, operating on a military schedule; and without warning, you are running late for every appointment, wearing two different shoes. Your relationship seems to have a bright future, and then you are unexpectedly broken-hearted, wondering what went wrong. Girls' night out with your besties happens regularly, until you discover pictures of another evening and do not understand why you were not invited. Your angelic child throws a tantrum of such epic proportions that you start thinking an exorcism might be in order.

Or one minute, you are walking into church with your family, minding your own business; the next, you are clinging to a handrail and pondering which will kill you first—the inevitable fall or the humiliation. Perhaps a more general way to say it is that, one minute, everything is moving along as planned; the next, you feel as though you shifted into reverse. It is difficult enough to feel as though you are stuck and struggling to get where you want to go; however, moving backward and feeling you are losing every bit of ground you gained is terrifying!

All through high school and college, I drove a bright red Monte Carlo that used more oil and transmission fluid than gas. I lost count of how many rebuilt transmissions I put in that car before I finished school. One day during my college years, I found myself broken down on the side of the road about a mile from home. The transmission had, once again, gone out, and no amount of fluid was going to help. The good news was that the car would drive in reverse (just not forward). How is this good news, you ask? Well, I had no money to pay for a tow, so I could leave the car there—which meant it would be stripped of anything that could be sold—or drive it home in reverse.

Oh yes, I did. I figured if God can make a way through the sea and a path through the mighty waters, surely He can make a reverse-moving lane down Pike Road. Nervous, scared, and embarrassed, I got behind the wheel, backed into the left lane, and prayed I could make it home without causing a major traffic jam. As it turns out, I did. Nobody died, and that car, sporting yet another rebuilt transmission, got me back and forth to school until I finished my degree and could buy something more reliable. This story is funny to me now, but I could not find the humor in it that day.

The world is dark; life is tough; and you will face challenges you never anticipated. Jesus said, "I am the light of the world. Whoever follows me will never walk in darkness, but will have the light of life" (John 8:12). Just like me, sitting on the side of the road, you have a choice: believe God will light your path and make a way or sit in the darkness, never knowing all He has in store for you.

I did not merely make it home safely that day; I learned to persevere when life gets tough. I learned to be strong and courageous when facing a giant and to let His light shine in the darkness to show my way. My time in reverse moved me forward faster than if I were driving in the Daytona 500.

If you are like me, when you feel yourself falling backward, you dig in your heels, then scrape and claw like a wildcat, falling down a steep cliff, trying your best to get back to where you felt safe and comfortable. Sometimes, God takes you out of your safe place in order to mold you into the woman He created you to be and prepare you for the future He planned for you. Sometimes, He pulls you back, so He can propel you forward. He knows what He is doing; you have to trust, even when you feel you are losing ground. You can bet that if you stay in His light, you will plunge forward at speeds you never thought possible.

Several years ago, my husband, Danny, lost his job of fifteen years. The company closed, and he was left with the task of starting over at the age of thirty-eight—not an easy task. For two years, he often worked two jobs, getting paid far beneath his value. When he was not working, he was sleeping. This time was difficult for us, but he was determined to hold on until God answered his prayer and provided a better job.

It was so hard to see the man I love work so much. I prayed for God to provide him the perfect job, one he loved that paid what he was worth. In the meantime, walking in faith and believing with everything in me that God would answer, I struggled to pay the bills. I look back now and wonder how in the world I managed as long as I did. I learned quickly how to borrow from Peter to pay Paul; but eventually, this practice catches up with you. I got behind on the mortgage; and eventually, there was no Peter to borrow from. We were about to lose the house.

The mortgage company gave me a deadline, or the house would go into foreclosure. I was out of options and had no idea what to do. I put down the phone, fell on the floor, and cried out to God— pleading, begging, defeated.

After some time of wallowing in misery, still sobbing on the floor, I heard the Lord say, "Kathy, will you serve Me, anyway?"

I immediately stopped crying. *What? Did I hear what I think I heard?*

Again, He said, "Will you serve Me, anyway?"

I knew my Savior was asking if my love and service to Him were conditional. Of course, I will love and serve Him if He delivers me. But what if He does not? What if we lose our home and face humiliation and defeat?

My reply was not long in coming. I whispered, "Yes, I will, Lord." Then I said it a little louder. "Yes, I will, Lord." I got to my feet and yelled, "I will serve You, Lord, no matter what!" I walked through the house, repeating over and over, "I will serve You, Lord, no matter what!"

I meant it. My love and service to my Father are not conditional. They are not based on what He can do for me because His love for me is not conditional. He sent His Son to die for me, so I can have a relationship with Him on this earth and live with Him for eternity! Even when I disobey Him, even when I fail Him, He never stops loving me.

We managed to get the mortgage caught up but not before it was posted in the foreclosure section of the local paper. At first, I was humiliated. Through a lot of prayer, however, I realized it does not matter what other people think and say. Their words have no power over me. Even at this low point, I realized how blessed I am to have such an amazing husband and family, and I was learning what a true relationship with my Father should be.

The story did not end there. The mortgage was current for the time being, but the problem remained. The bills and income were still the same. I continued to pray that God would provide the job with the income, adding each time, "But I will serve You, Lord, no matter what."

While Danny kept working at both jobs, I looked for a second job. We were waiting on God's provision, but we did not sit back to wait for a check in the mail. (Although, I have to admit, I did pray for that kind of miracle.) We kept working, looking, and doing everything we could to help ourselves—and then came a glimmer of hope. Danny received a call about a great job he had applied for, and the first step was passing a test in reading and math. The reading portion was a nonissue; but the math, mostly algebra, was a different story. My husband is a smart man; but like many of us, math was not his best subject, and he had never taken an algebra class. "There is no way I can pass a test on something I never learned," he said. Remembering Philippians 4:13, I replied, "You can do all things through Christ."

The day of the test, we solely and completely believed in God's intervention. Danny called me right before and asked, "Do you think I should even bother?" The enemy knew God was working and wanted to stop it. I encouraged him to go take that test and trust God for the outcome. Either way, God is faithful, and we would be okay. We hung up, and I hit my knees.

A few hours later, Danny called and laughingly said, "I have never seen most of the math on that test."

I simply answered, "God has."

Danny passed the test and went for the interview. In the meantime, waiting to hear if he was hired, I received a call about teaching online courses part-time for a college. I sent them my information and interviewed, and we waited to hear about both jobs. On a Saturday, Danny received a call from a friend who had gone through the hiring process with him. He was reporting to orientation the following Tuesday. Danny had not been contacted and was convinced he would not be hired. I tried to reassure him, but I could almost hear Satan's whisper in his ear. I encouraged him to call the recruiter, but Danny said he would not be in the office on a Saturday. He carried the weight of the world on his shoulders. I hit my knees again, so angry at how the enemy was doing everything he could to discourage my husband. I knew God had a plan and prayed He would not allow Danny to go another day without knowing what it was.

The best part of the story is how our time became God's time. Within minutes, Danny said, "You won't believe this."

He had called the recruiter, who did answer the phone on a Saturday and told Danny that yes, he was going to be hired and that he had planned to call him on Monday. He also mentioned that he was normally not in the office on Saturday but had stopped by to get something. God popped the enemy right on the head, lifted that burden from Danny's shoulders, and made sure we knew it was Him! He is worthy to be praised!

Not only did God show up that day, but He also showed out! On the same day Danny received the official phone call, the college hired me to teach the online classes. God not only gave us back the income we lost, but He also gave us more! His provision did not end there. Two years later, I was promoted to assistant principal—increased income. A year later, I became the principal—increased income. God gave us the income we lost and then some, and then He blessed us beyond anything we ever dreamed.

I am not ashamed to tell you we went through a hard financial crisis and nearly lost our home. I am also not ashamed to tell you that in His time, God delivered us from that crisis and gave us more than we asked! It was unbelievable! It was miraculous! It was God!

Can you see how one day we were moving forward financially and then suddenly went into reverse, feeling as though we were losing everything? God had a plan for us—not to harm us but to prosper us (Jer. 29:11). If my husband had not lost his job, would he have pursued one for which he doubted his qualifications? Would I have looked into part-time, remote teaching if we were not struggling financially? We probably would not have; but as life pulled us backward, God was getting us ready to push forward.

Times like these are hard. If God asked for volunteers of people who want to be pulled back in order to move forward, I doubt anyone would raise a hand! When you feel He has forsaken you, that He does not care, or that you will never overcome, know He is working. In this fallen world, you will encounter dark times. When you choose to walk in His light and commit to serve Him, no matter what, you will overcome the darkness brought on by fear and unforgiveness and learn how to keep walking, knowing your steps are ordered.

CROWN EFFECT 7
Overcome the Darkness of Fear

I REMEMBER THE DAY WE brought our first baby home from the hospital. I watched my husband place her perfect, tiny body into a Federal Aviation Administration-approved car seat, secured by a Road Safety Authority-approved seatbelt, rear-facing in the back seat of a car recognized by the Insurance Institute for Highway Safety as one of the safest vehicles on the road. And then it descended—an overwhelming, I-cannot-move, I-cannot-breathe, can-we-just-stay-at-the-hospital—fear. Every "what if" scenario played through my mind like a YouTube video. For decades, parents drove with infants in their laps, toddlers standing up next to them in the front seat, and thought nothing of it.

We had invested in the safest vehicle we could hardly afford, yet I was gripped with terror. It did not matter that the car was one of the safest on the road. It did not matter that she was in one of the best car seats. I was afraid!

The fear did not end there, and giving birth to our second child only added to my anxiety. Thoughts of terrible things that could happen invaded my mind, and I sat down and cried—not over what did happen but what could. My intelligent mind told me how stupid it was and that I needed to get over it. But how? I did not want to have those thoughts. They just came to me, uninvited and unwelcome.

We are all afraid at times; but being gripped with fear that steals your time, peace, and joy is like being held captive against your will—fighting an enemy you cannot see. Ephesians 6:12 says, "For our struggle is not against flesh and blood, but against the rulers, against the authorities, against the powers of this dark world and against the spiritual forces of evil in the heavenly realms." Who are these principalities, powers, and rulers of darkness? We all know the answer: Satan and his battalion of fallen angels, our enemy.

Sun Tzu, one of the greatest military strategists, said, "Know thy enemy and know yourself; in a hundred battles, you will never be defeated." The *know yourself* part is easy to understand; we covered it in chapter one. Let us be honest, though. The idea of knowing Satan, ruler of darkness, can incite fear, and you may find yourself avoiding the subject completely. Jesus understands. He dealt with Satan face to face, taunted by him at one of the weakest moments in His life on earth. Imagine how frail He felt in his human form after fasting forty days and nights. Satan took advantage of what he thought would be Jesus' vulnerability, and he does the same to us.

Anytime we are weak or vulnerable, the enemy tries to use it to pull us away from God or to keep us from doing what God has called us to do. For this reason, as Sun Tzu said, we must recognize the enemy and know how to resist him. Have you noticed most of the advertisements that pop up on your devices relate to things that interest you—possibly even something you recently searched? It is not a coincidence. Advertisers place targeting cookies on websites to gather information about you and use it to influence what you see.

Satan has cookies, too! (And they are not drizzled with chocolate syrup and covered in sprinkles.) With help from his minions, he prowls around, watching, listening, and gathering information about you. What are your fears, insecurities, and desires? What do you battle physically or emotionally? When he has the information he needs, he designs a marketing plan for one purpose: to sell you a lie.

If his advertisements appeared on your timeline or newsfeed, they might say that if you made mistakes in your past, you can wear this burden for the rest of your life because no one will ever forgive you. If you are past forty and have yet to reach your goals, give up and drink this cup of misery every day for the rest of your life. If you have not lost the weight, eat a spoonful of self-doubt and loathing every day until no one wants to be around you, anyway. If you are not right beside your children all the time, something bad will happen to them. If you fall and flash the church congregation, head for the door and never show your face in that place again.

Do those ideas sound familiar? The enemy's marketing aims to fill your head with doubt, rip apart your self-esteem, and take away your joy. He wants to deceive, destroy, and devour you—but you know him. You know his messages are lies, and you have the freedom to choose whether or not to buy what he sells. When the enemy tempted Jesus, He did not flinch. He was not afraid because He immediately recognized His enemy, and He knew how to defeat him. Jesus knew Satan has no power over the Word of God, so He responded with it all three times the enemy came at Him with a temptation.

When I had my children, the enemy saw an opportunity. He knew being a new mom comes with a lot of vulnerability and responsibility, so he devised a plan to consume me with fear, bringing darkness to what should have been the most joyful season of my life. But he only had what power I gave him, so I chose to walk in the light and took his power away. Your Father does not want you to live in fear. He repeatedly tells us not to be afraid throughout His Word. He does not say, "Try not to be afraid." He says, "Do not."

We all experience fear at some point, and it can be overwhelming and sometimes debilitating, stealing our peace, joy, plans, and purpose. If we recognize Satan as the source of the darkness and focus on the truth of God's Word, we can overcome fear and walk in peace, knowing God is always in control.

CROWN EFFECT 8
Find the Light of Forgiveness

I NEVER KNEW WHAT UNFORGIVENESS was until I realized I had not forgiven someone for doing something I could not even remember her doing. My baby girl was shy, but oh-so-sassy and demanding, and Mommy was her person—the center of her universe. She would not stay with anyone but her babysitter and grandparents and, at this time, refused to stay away from home overnight. Against every parenting book I read, she fell asleep every night, nestled in the curve of my arm until she started school. Pacifiers, particular blankets, and favorite stuffed animals never captivated her because I was her security. She wanted only me and, to be honest, nearly sucked the life right out of me! I never got a break. During meals, baths, and bedtimes, it was always, "Mommy do it." She wanted no one but me to do anything for her.

One day when she was five, the same age I was when my mother gave me up, something happened out of the blue. I do not know what triggered it or why; it could have been some deep-rooted psychological meltdown, worthy of professional evaluation, or perhaps some sick and twisted plot of the enemy. Whatever it was, I began to see my five-year-old self in my daughter—a little girl who depended so much on her mommy, cuddling close as she fell asleep at night. I could see her, sitting on Mommy's lap and covering her ears to hide from a thunderstorm. She felt most secure in her mommy's arms. And then I could only see her alone. Her mommy was gone.

At age thirty-two, I began to mourn for that sweet five-year-old, whose world was shattered. How scared she must have been! How her heart must have broken, wondering what she had done wrong! Angry, I asked how my mother could give up her children. I did not want to spend one night away from mine, and she chose to spend the rest of her life away from hers. Who does that?

Soon, the darkness crept in, and the enemy would have loved nothing more than to steal my joy and keep me from being the mother my children needed me to be. He wanted me to walk in hurt, bitterness, anger, and unforgiveness. But Jesus made it clear that forgiveness is not an option. If we want to receive grace, we must give it. If we want mercy, we must be merciful ourselves. If we want to be forgiven, we must forgive. I had to learn how to forgive someone who had not asked for my forgiveness. To do that, I had to understand why she left my brother and me.

One of fourteen children, my mother grew up extremely poor, had a tough mother and alcoholic father, and was forced to leave home at age fourteen merely to survive. As a result, she was a fighter. She once drew blood from the neck of stepdad number two with a simple flick of her nail—his punishment for mentioning another woman during a card game with friends. His ex-wife soon regretted coming to their apartment to start trouble when, panther-like, Mom moved in, snatched that woman up by the hair of her head, and dragged her to the ground before she knew what hit her!

Although she had a hard time expressing love and building positive relationships, she certainly knew how to fight for anyone she loved. Sadly, she was filled with so much pain and anger that she could never see herself as anything other than a victim and a fighter. Her anger grew, manifesting itself anywhere, toward anyone. One by one, she severed every relationship she had, including with friends and family, but I loved her. She was my mother. She gave me life. Unfortunately, she was damaged and had not allowed Jesus to heal her heart and put her broken pieces back together.

The Bible says, "All have sinned and fall short of the glory of God" (Rom. 3:23). *All* includes me. I am no better than my mother, but I am forgiven because God sent His Son to shed His blood and die on the cross. If my heavenly Father can forgive me, who am I to withhold forgiveness? Regardless of circumstance, pain, or excuse, if I want to be forgiven, I must forgive.

I forgave my mother for giving me away. I forgave her for not being there when I needed someone to help me the first time I shaved my legs, put on makeup, and started puberty. I forgave her for not being there for my first day of school, first date, and my first break-up. I forgave her for missing my school plays, ball games, and graduation. I forgave her because my Savior forgave me. It was one of the most difficult things I have ever done.

Exercising forgiveness is hard, both saying the words and actually meaning them. Besides Jesus telling us to forgive, though, we have another reason to do so: unforgiveness causes darkness. Looking into her past, I realized quickly that my mother was hurt by her own parents; and having never found forgiveness, she lived a life of bitterness and hatred. If I did not forgive her, I would become like her, walking through life in darkness, bitter and depressed over what was not. I chose to break the generational curse of anger and bitterness, to walk in the light of forgiveness, and to be the mother to my daughter and son that God called me to be.

CROWN EFFECT 9
Keep Walking, Knowing Your Steps Are Ordered

I OFTEN WONDER HOW IN the world my brother and I turned out well (depending, of course, on one's definition of well)! Like many other children, the odds were against us. Satan had more than enough ammunition to use against us—and I think he used it all—but we made it. We overcame. We broke the chains and escaped the pain, finding peace and hope, because of one woman—Mammaw.

Mammaw endured many hardships, but she never flinched. Once I became a wife and mother and could truly appreciate the sacrifices she had made for us, I wrote to her, sharing my heart and thanking her for the life she had given us. In my mind, this letter was a long time coming; but she called me in tears, completely surprised by my words. She did not consider taking us in to be a sacrifice; it was a gift from God. She trusted her Father completely and believed when He said, "'For I know the plans I have for you'" (Jer. 29:11). She knew when those five- and seven-year-olds arrived on her doorstep, confused and afraid, that God had a plan.

During challenging times in my life, she would always say, "Keep walking. Your steps are ordered." While I was a bright student, no one really noticed. Now, as an educator, I often wonder how I could consistently score in the ninety-ninth percentile on standardized tests each year without ever being encouraged to take advanced placement courses or prepare for college. I was overlooked, graduating high school without cords, medals, honors, scholarships, or a plan.

Working in a church youth camp after graduation, I received a call from my high school business and typing teacher. Her husband, an attorney, needed a secretary, and I could type sixty-five words per minute. Eighteen and scared, I started my first job as a legal secretary the next week, remembering Mammaw's words. "Keep walking. Your steps are ordered."

This job was a great start; but my coworkers at youth camp were headed to college, and I wanted to join them. Dreaming of more and determined to get there, I convinced my grandmother to let me go and proceeded to learn how to fill out applications and financial aid forms. Then I loaded my Monte Carlo—the one that drank more oil than gas—and drove myself to college.

On move-in day, all the other girls had parents with them to haul boxes and decorate dorm rooms. I was alone, and everything I owned fit in the back seat of my car. I would love to describe how brilliantly I did and how successful I was, but my first semester's 1.75 grade point average tells a different story—I was not prepared and was clueless about how to study or what degree I wanted to pursue, and I had fallen in love with a boy back home. After two semesters, I packed up the Monte Carlo, embarrassed and disappointed.

I transferred to a school closer to home with a much bigger purpose in mind—getting married. Sometimes, we just need the right motivation. A tall, muscular, good-looking blond with a kind heart and love for Jesus was all the incentive I needed to tackle a full load, complete with summer classes and mini-terms, and graduate in three years with a degree in business education, the same degree held by the teacher who helped me get the job as a legal secretary. All I lacked was a teaching position; but the school year was about to start, and no openings existed. Discouraged, I focused on Mammaw's advice. "Keep walking. Your steps are ordered."

Just before our wedding, a teacher in the school system where we were going to live passed away suddenly. The ripple effect of filling his classroom opened a position for me, and I started at Cordova High School the day after we returned from our honeymoon. For the next twenty-two years, I taught, coached softball, sponsored clubs, decorated proms, rode in homecoming parades, and served on hundreds of committees and leadership teams—birthing and bringing up two children of my own in the meantime.

When my children were old enough to drive, aspirations of a pay raise prompted me to work toward a master's degree in educational leadership. For the sake of my pride, let the record here show that I achieved a 3.9 grade point average in the program—a far cry from my humble beginning of 1.75. (Hopefully, you now feel better about my educating children for more than three decades!) Eventually, I became the assistant principal and then head principal of the school—a tremendous responsibility. I was terrified but remembered what Mammaw said: "Keep walking. Your steps are ordered."

Retiring from a career of thirty-two years was not easy. I was sad to leave that part of my life and uncertain of what the future might hold. Five months later, I started writing a book, excited but so overwhelmed by the idea that I could hardly say it out loud. Was it possible that I could be a published author? I chose to keep walking.

God has a plan for your life. He formed you in the womb and knew you before you were born. Your steps are ordered. When you are overlooked, scared, alone, embarrassed, disappointed, discouraged, exhausted, terrified, uncertain, or overwhelmed, just keep walking. I do not know what comes next—none of us does—but I do know that our steps are ordered. As long as we keep walking in His light, we will never walk in darkness.

Pause For Reflection

Have you ever felt as though you are losing ground or moving in the wrong direction? How did you respond? _____

_____

_____

_____

_____

_____

Did God use the trials in your life to teach, strengthen, and refine you? If so, give an example of a time He used a difficult season to make you more like Him. _____

_____

_____

_____

_____

_____

_____

Do you sometimes question God when life gets hard, and He does not seem to hear your cries? If so, write a verse here that you can use to combat this thought the next time the enemy whispers his lies in your ear. _____

_____

_____

_____

Have you walked in the darkness of fear? If so, write a verse here that you can use to focus on God's strength in the future.

_____

_____

_____

"For our struggle is not against flesh and blood, but against the rulers, against the authorities, against the powers of this dark world and against the spiritual forces of evil in the heavenly realms."

Ephesians 6:12

Do you recognize Satan, the enemy, when he attacks? _____

_____

_____

_____

Why is it important to know the source of your fear? _____

_____

_____

_____

How does unforgiveness cause darkness? _____

_____

_____

"For if you forgive other people when they sin against you, your
heavenly Father will also forgive you. But if you do not forgive others
their sins, your Father will not forgive your sins."

Matthew 6:14-15

What does this Scripture say about a child of God who walks in the
darkness of unforgiveness? _____

_____

_____

_____

What steps can you take to forgive someone who hurt you? _____

_____

_____

_____

What does "keep walking; your steps are ordered" mean to you? ____

_____

_____

_____

Are you fully committed to serving God, no matter what? _____

_____

_____

CHAPTER 4
Live the Best Life Possible

IF YOU RECALL, THIS STORY started the day I thought life was as good as it gets and then found myself dangling upside down, holding on for everything I was worth. Our best life is not an ideal one. This beautiful time God gives us, surrounded by beautiful people in a beautiful world, is filled with chaos and uncertainty. At some point, we will walk through a storm, enter a valley, stand in the fire, face a giant, or fight a battle; we do not have to do it alone.

During a busy season over twenty years ago, I was a teacher with two young children, and my husband was out of town for work. The one person who loved me sacrificially and unconditionally all my life, my mammaw, lay in the hospital with congestive heart failure. I was torn, wanting to sit at the hospital with her around the clock. We did not know how long she would be there, but we never dreamed she would not go home again.

I took off work to spend time talking, laughing, and loving on her. She was such a strong woman, always caring for others, never putting her needs ahead of anyone else's. That day, she let me pamper her; I rubbed lotion on her dry skin and brushed and braided her hair. She laughed at the sight of an eighty-four-year-old woman in braids. I sat on the side of her bed, wishing I could crawl up and hold on to her forever. I had no idea why I felt so drawn to her, but God did.

Several days later, we learned she was septic and being treated with large amounts of antibiotics. We had family with her around the clock, and I had children to care for and a classroom of students to teach. Still, I wanted to be there myself. On a morning when the struggle between going in to work or taking yet another day for a hospital visit was particularly hard, I prayed for guidance, yielded to the sense of urgency, and headed to the hospital. As I pulled into the parking deck, the call to drop everything came from my cousin. How blessed I was to already be there! I had no idea that it was the day she would leave this earth, but God did.

We gathered around, watching the slow decline of her heart rate on the monitor. I held her hand and kissed her. I did not want her to leave me, but her chariot was waiting to take her to her Father. I could hear Him say, *"Well done, good and faithful servant! You have been faithful with a few things; I will put you in charge of many things. Come and share your master's happiness!"* (Matt. 25:21) She continued to hold on, like she did not want to let go. Unsure of what to do or say, I did not know what she needed from me, but God did.

The nurse told us that opinions vary as to whether an unresponsive person can hear at this stage; so, my precious cousin, Denise, sang, "Peace, Peace, Wonderful Peace"—Mammaw's favorite. As Denise's voice filled the room, it seemed Mammaw might not have peace in leaving because she had unfinished business: my dad, her baby boy.

She had cared for him, bailed him out of many bad situations—one might even say she had enabled him. She lived for her family and trusted God that they would all spend eternity in Heaven. Two of her children were already with the Lord, and one served Him faithfully; but my dad struggled.

Still holding her hand, I whispered in her ear, "If you are ready to go be with the Lord, it is okay. You can go. I promise I will take care of your baby."

A tear rolled down her face. Within minutes, she was in the presence of her Savior. God knew that the promise her son would not be alone was what she needed to hear. Until the day he left this earth, my dad would say, "You know, Momma always told me the Lord was not going to let me miss Heaven."

Deuteronomy 7:9 says, "Know therefore that the Lord your God is God; he is the faithful God, keeping his covenant of love to a thousand generations of those who love him and keep his commandments." This truth is not a complicated one. If you love God and keep His commandments, He will be faithful to you. He will calm the storm, pull you out of the valley, stand in the fire with you, slay your giant, and fight your battles. You will face tough times, but He will be there. When you are grieving, He will be your Comfort. When you are weak, He will be your Strength. When you are lost, He will be your Guide. When you are afraid, He will be your Peace. When you are sick, He will be your Healer.

He will be faithful and do what He says He will do in His time. If you think about it, though, the problem is not His time. It is the meantime—you know, that time between your first asking God for something and when you actually get an answer. It is that time when the enemy gets in your face, whispers in your ear, belittles your faith, and tries to steal your joy. It is that time when tears come to your eyes, fear grips your heart, hope fades, and you find yourself binge-watching Netflix while consuming a half gallon of ice cream, topped with cookie crumbles. The *meantime* is hard, and the word itself says it all—it can feel as though God is being mean.

Remember that deathbed promise to my grandmother? While it was easy to make in the moment, I had no way of knowing what keeping it would entail. My dad was an alcoholic. When Mammaw passed away, he still lived on his own and spent most of his time in bars. I kept in touch with him, encouraged him to control his drinking, and invited him to family gatherings. He usually came to my house on Thanksgiving and Christmas but never stayed long because spending time with us made him need a drink to numb his guilt and regret.

Two things make an alcoholic's life miserable. The need for alcohol holds complete control over him. As a result, he lives in constant guilt for the pain it causes others, deeply regretting what could have or should have been in the time lost to his addiction. Alcoholism steals so much from a person that can never be reclaimed, particularly time. I honestly believed at that point in his life my dad might try to stop drinking, if not for the pain of a wasted life, broken relationships, disappointments, loneliness, and deep sadness.

When my dad eventually encountered money trouble, his brother took him in, got him cleaned up, took him to doctors' appointments, entertained him, and helped him get back on his feet financially. The situation was great for my dad but did not last long. Dad called me to come get him, and it began—the *meantime*.

Moving him to a house near me worked well until the heavy drinking began. We endured several extended hospital and nursing facility admissions due to heart problems, falls, and weakness from malnutrition and dehydration. The twenty-one-day stays in the nursing facility were tough. Of course, drinking was prohibited, and he could smoke only during scheduled, escorted walks outside. He was miserable. Keeping him from leaving on his own took a lot of effort.

After each rehabilitation period, I took him home; and we started over. He always regretted the situations he created and promised to do better. Watching someone live with addiction is heartbreaking. While I have resented my dad for the pain he caused at times, he was not a bad person. I do not excuse him because he chose a life that contradicted his upbringing and led to addiction, but he had a big heart. He would give his last dollar to anyone who asked (a trait that led to his being taken advantage of often). He loved his mother more than any other person in his world. Most importantly, he loved God.

Drinking finally made him sick enough to realize he was killing himself, and I convinced him to eliminate the whiskey and have beer only, promising I would keep his refrigerator stocked. He agreed, demanding beer, popcorn, and ice cream, regardless of what other food was in the house. Obviously, this diet is not heart-healthy, and many people asked why I let him have beer. At the time, he was in his seventies and had been drinking and smoking for sixty years. He was going to get it if he had to crawl to the store himself. My goal was to prevent his hurting himself or others and to minimize the damage to his body.

One day, he got mad at me for refusing to get his car fixed. Simply put, I could not let him drive. In anger, he turned against me. He fired Becky—his longtime, longsuffering caregiver—and declared his friend would look after him. Furious, I warned him the decision was a mistake, and he would live with the consequences he chose. I would love my dad, check on him, and be his family; however, I could no longer take care of him.

In less than two months, he was back in the hospital and rehabilitation, forcing a decision upon me—to walk away or to resume caring for this homebound man, who could do nothing for himself but expect an endless supply of beer, popcorn, and ice cream. I was torn. Everyone agreed that my walking away was justified. Yes, I loved him, but he did not raise me. My grandparents were my parents, and we cared for and buried them years ago. The situation was unfair, emotionally draining, and caused so much resentment to rise up in me. I wanted to walk in forgiveness. I wanted peace; at the same time, my insides screamed, "How long must I carry the burden of his sins?"

One night, I prayed myself to sleep over the situation, waking several times to ask God to show me what to do. Around 3:30 a.m., I heard the Lord say, "This is not about him. This is not about you. It is about your grandmother and her faithfulness. This is the answer to her prayers." I was not caring for my dad because of my promise but because of God's promise in answer to the powerful prayer of a faithful servant, my grandmother. Although she was gone from this earth, her prayers lived on, which explained why I never had peace over leaving. I continued to do my best, and God was faithful. Dad died alone at home. Because of my grandmother's prayers to our faithful, loving God, I know He was there.

Many people face addiction in the family. It is tough. No guidebooks and little help exist. Addiction breaks your heart, enrages you, makes you want to run away, hurts to the core, and leaves scars. Jesus said, "'With man this is impossible, but with God all things are possible'" (Matt. 19:26). Life is hard; and sometimes, we have to do things we think we cannot or do not want to do. However, if we trust God and obey, He will always make a way in His time. In the meantime, He gives strength to persevere, even when that means buying an endless supply of beer, popcorn, and ice cream or pulling yourself up after an embarrassing fall.

Living your best life is not about living a perfect life; it is facing each day with a hopeful heart, living in sweet surrender, and believing that God has a planned purpose for you. It is about getting through the meantime while waiting on His perfect time.

CROWN EFFECT 10
Begin Each Day With a Hopeful Heart

HAVE YOU EVER LONGED FOR something with a desire in your heart so strong it consumes you? You think about it all the time, dream about it every night, and pray about it every day. As a child, I longed for a family. Although I lived with grandparents who loved me very much, I spent my entire childhood, dreaming of having a family that was not shattered by divorce, abandonment, and addiction. I tuned in to *The Brady Bunch,* aching for the corny, cheesy, dull, old-fashioned, sappy story of the perfect family. Watching fairy tales prompts most girls to dream of riding off into the sunset with the handsome prince; I wished a strong, loving dad would come rescue me and yearned for a mom to take me shopping and help with my hair and makeup.

My childhood family dynamic remained unchanged, but God heard me and answered my prayer in His time. As a teenager, I attended the annual Church of God camp meeting in June. The open-door tabernacle had no air conditioning, but it was fine because I was not there for the service and never once set foot inside the building. Like several other girls, I was there for the boys. True, we should have been in the service, hearing the Word of God, but we figured we could do worse than look for a boyfriend at the church.

Years of participating in the manhunt finally brought success on the first night of meeting when I was nineteen. I was not the prettiest girl there but knew deep inside I was special and had something to offer. Anyone would be lucky to date me; he simply had yet to realize it! I believed I was who God said I was. I noticed one young man in particular—a tall, blue-eyed blond with a dark tan, huge muscles, and impressive mullet—glancing my way several times that night, so I shyly looked away, feigning disinterest. I may not have dated in a while; but if he wanted to go out with me, he needed to work for it. I am royalty!

I informed my cousin with grand assurance that we would go out by the end of the week; she was unconvinced. My confident prediction rang true, though. In a few days, we were on our first date. I fell head over heels in love with him. He was beautiful; he genuinely loved the Lord; and he could have any girl he wanted. He chose me! How did that happen? God saw that young girl with the hopeful heart, and He answered her prayer. We have been married nearly forty years, have two children and a daughter-in-law, and the grandchildren have begun to arrive.

I would love to tell you how perfect life has been, but it would not be true. We have hard times. We get on each other's nerves. The man will not stop smacking his gum, and he leaves every light in the house turned on behind him like a path back to where he started. I drive my clean car through every mud hole and run the gas tank completely empty. We will never agree on everything, but we know some things for sure. We love one another. Our union was an answer to prayer. Our marriage was God's plan, and He is the Ruler over our home. We will serve Him, no matter what.

God is good, and He is faithful. He loves and sees you. No matter what is happening in your life right now, what you face, what you long for or need, He is there. No matter how long you have waited, He is working, even when your faith is weak.

The Bible tells a beautiful story in 2 Kings 4:8-37 of the woman from Shunem. I believe it reveals how God, in His glorious grace, uses our struggle to grow our faith. She lived with her husband and had no children but helped God's prophet Elisha by giving him food and a room when he passed through town. In return for her kindness, Elisha asked what he could give her. A wealthy woman, she replied that she was content and wanted nothing.

Her husband's age could indicate that she gave up hope of conceiving, choosing contentment with her circumstances as they stood. While she loved and honored God, perhaps she underestimated what He would do for her. As a result, she never mentioned to the prophet that she was childless and wanted a son, but God knew. When Elisha told her she would have a son, she replied, "'No, my lord . . . Please, man of God, don't mislead your servant'" (2 Kings 4:16). Not only had she given up hope of having a son, but she was also afraid to consider it might even be possible. "'With God, all things are possible'" (Matt. 19:26). In time, she bore a son.

Years later, her son died in her arms. Can you imagine receiving a miracle from God—one you dared not hope for, far less request—only to have it taken away by tragedy? But the woman's faith had grown.

She had witnessed what God could do and learned not to doubt Him. Wasting no time, she went to Elisha and fell at his feet. "'Did I ask you for a son, my lord?' she said. 'Didn't I tell you, *Don't raise my hopes?*'" (2 Kings 4:28) Having birthed a son after years of waiting in vain, only to lose him in an unexpected, untimely death, is a heavy weight to bear, even for one who puts all her trust in God. As always, God was faithful. Elisha went to the child and restored his life.

Our best life in this fallen world is sometimes messy and chaotic. You will endure trials and tribulations, storms and valleys. You may even fall down the church stairs, but never underestimate what God can and will do. The Bible says, "Out of his fullness we have all received grace in place of grace already given" (John 1:16). God's gift of grace is abundant and unending. It is like receiving a boundless supply of birthday presents. Who does not love birthday presents? Living your best possible life means beginning each day with hope and excitement about what you know God will do.

CROWN EFFECT 11
Live Each Day in Sweet Surrender

IN THE 1960S AND '70S, my family drove big cars. My first memory of riding in a car is actually the only one I have of my parents being together. They took my brother and me to a drive-in movie that I cannot name because it was apparently not for children, as we were restricted to the backseat floorboard. We camped out down there with blankets and pillows, toys and games, popcorn and candy, oblivious to the mature storyline that played on the big screen. We were so caught up in our backseat adventure that even the blaring speakers failed to catch our attention.

Living with my grandparents showed me what a big car really is. That Buick LaSabre transported us to so many fond childhood memories—my brother and I, wedged between our grandparents up front, with at least four cousins squashed in the back, headed to the lake or some other family outing. PawPaw was a terrible driver, and any trip with him involved a lot of cursing, while Mammaw either cried out to the Lord or breathed, "Jesus, Jesus, Jesus." Pawpaw thought nothing of squeezing between two cars on a two-lane road, even if it meant taking some paint as he passed. Of course, none of us wore seatbelts. When Pawpaw hit the brakes (which he did often), Mammaw threw her arm across my chest to keep my head from slamming into the radio, yelling, "Help us, Jesus!" while the cousins ended in a pile on the floorboard in back. It was during those times that I learned both what it means to surrender every day to God and, thanks to Mammaw, how to cry out to God for His mercy, protection, and peace.

Mammaw was a homemaker with a seventh-grade education. She raised four of her own children and the two of us, cooked and cleaned, and tended to her husband's every need until he took his last breath. Her father was a Pentecostal preacher, so she never wore a pair of pants or a swipe of makeup; and her long hair was always pulled back in a bun. Short and stocky, she never considered herself to be physically attractive, but I can attest that having my mammaw in your life was to know the smartest, most beautiful woman on this earth. No one ever came to her house without feeling loved. If you did not know about Jesus when you met her, you did when you left. One day, the Sears and Roebuck appliance repairman came to fix her broken oven. The entire time he worked, she shared salvation with him. He left a changed man!

Mammaw walked with God every day and filled the house with prayer and song as she spent her days cooking and cleaning. As I grew older, I came to understand that the hymn "Peace, Peace, Wonderful Peace" was her anthem, her survival, her hope. She lived each day in full and complete surrender to God. She surrendered her husband; I heard her praising God in her bedroom the day he died. Having surrendered her children, she praised Him at their funerals. She surrendered her finances and offered praise even when bills could not be paid. On the day she moved in with her son, she praised God as they drove away from the home she had surrendered. Recovering from open heart surgery, she lay in her bed and praised Him because she surrendered her health, too. She surrendered her life, so I know she praised God when she went to be with the Lord.

While Mammaw's life was hard sometimes, she enjoyed the blessings of a sixty-year marriage, four children, eleven grandchildren, and twenty-one great grandchildren—every one of whom call her blessed. The family gathered in a cousin's home after her funeral to eat a meal the church prepared for us. Surrounded by loved ones in the kitchen as we had done so many times before, I was overcome with grief because she was not there with us. I could barely breathe, far less eat. She would have so loved to bustle around in the middle of it all! How could I go on without her? I took a deep breath and began to praise God, just like she would have done. I surrendered it all to Him—loss, pain, grief. I made it through that day and every one since then, doing what I learned from her—praising God.

One of the Bible's greatest examples of complete surrender to God is the story of Job. God Himself described Job as "'blameless and upright, a man who fears God and shuns evil'" (Job 1:8). In spite of his goodness, he suffered when God gave Satan permission to persecute him. In one day, he lost everything—his servants, his animals, and his children. Imagine his pain and sorrow, devastation, loss, and grief. He must have felt hurt that God allowed these things to happen.

We read that he "got up and tore his robe and shaved his head. Then he fell to the ground in worship" (Job 1:20). Such a response seems almost unfathomable. How could he worship immediately after receiving news that he had lost his wealth and his children at the same time? The passage continues with Job's declaration. "'Naked I came from my mother's womb, and naked I will depart. The Lord gave and the Lord has taken away; may the name of the Lord be praised'" (Job 1:21). Fully surrendered to God, he knew everything he had belonged to God, so he worshipped and praised the name of the Lord.

Job's battle did not end there. Next, he was afflicted with sores that covered his entire body, suffering to the point of wishing for death. Still, his faith did not waver. "'Though he slay me, yet will I hope in him'" (Job 13:15). Naturally, Job was discouraged. Surely, he questioned why this was happening to him, but he never gave up hope in God. What a great example to follow in the midst of battle when it feels like you can no longer continue! You can worship, regardless of how difficult the circumstances seem or how weak you become. Praise the God Who gives life, forgives, and loves unconditionally.

Job 42:10 says that "after Job had prayed for his friends, the Lord restored his fortunes and gave him twice as much as he had before." Job's hope rested firmly in the Lord, even though he did not know how his battle would end; and God rewarded his faithfulness with deliverance and restoration.

Your best life is lived in sweet surrender to your Father. Give your grief, pain, regret, sickness, worry, depression, and fear to God. If you pick it up again, as we sometimes do, give it back to Him.

CROWN EFFECT 12
Believe Each Day Is God's Planned Purpose For You

WHEN I FIRST MARRIED, I knew nothing about being a wife and running a household. My grandmother did a wonderful job of loving me and teaching me spiritually; but none of her practical instruction included what a healthy marriage looks like, budgeting and managing finances, or sex. On top of that, growing up with the best cook in America means you are rarely allowed in the kitchen during meal preparation.

Then came the children, both of whom were surprises. I may have dreamed of this family, but I had never bothered to learn about what to do when I got it. Lacking the technology available to new parents today, I was the baby monitor at night. I was terrified they would stop breathing in the night and broke all the rules. For the first two years of their lives, they slept right next to me in bed; I never made it through a single REM cycle. I overcompensated for everything, making sure they had all the things I missed as a child.

Birthday parties required all-night decorating, characters, costumes, food, music, dancing, party favors, hayrides, swimming, limousines, and any other idea I could find. Clark Griswold has nothing on my holiday celebrations—we were "gonna have the hap-hap-happiest Christmas" and every other holiday if it killed me. (It almost did!) I wanted to be the perfect mother, which reveals how imperfect I was. I was a mess.

At this point in life, one would think I have it all together: my children left the nest, I have a blog after retiring from an amazing career, and I am now a published author. However, I have yet to discover the key to a perfect marriage and still cannot cook. I worry about my children as much as I did when they were babies. I overcompensate, trying to make up for lost years. I still want every holiday to be epic. And to top it off, getting older brings a whole new set of insecurities, anxieties, and fears. I remain a mess.

Ironically, I look back to those first years of marriage and laugh, remembering how we left our first Christmas tree up until March because we were in a standoff after my husband made the mistake of saying it was my job to take down the tree! (Clearly, he had to learn a lesson.) The first meal I cooked was hamburgers and fries, which we ate cold after my husband, an only child, stopped by his parents' house on the way home. Once, we came home to no running water in the house. Apparently, they really do expect your bill to be paid on time.

Now, I can think of the mess and laugh. My heart smiles with the memory of snuggling up to those precious babies and listening to their hearts beat, even if it meant no sleep. Recalling their laughter at birthday parties, I know they felt special and loved when I felt exhausted. Their excitement over holiday decorating and anticipation for Santa radiated joy in the moments I was thinking, "It's Christmas, and we're all in misery."

I face each day with anticipation and excitement over what God has in store for my life in retirement. While my marriage remains an imperfect one, we share many wonderful memories of an imperfect life raising imperfect children, who still worry me but fill me with such pride, watching them build their own messy lives. I may stress over birthdays and holidays, but my children's insistence that we carry on every tradition warms my heart. I am getting older but would not trade one memory of my messy life to go back in time. God makes a mess into a masterpiece by using your perfect potential to fulfill His planned purpose for your life.

God can use your imperfections and wants you to learn from your mistakes. Regardless of where you have been, God went before you. Do not dwell on these circumstances; instead, dwell on Him. "For we are God's handiwork, created in Christ Jesus to do good works, which God prepared in advance for us to do" (Eph. 2:10). You are a work of God, created for a purpose He planned before you were born; you need only to believe it.

Pause For Reflection

"Know therefore that the Lord your God is God; he is the faithful God, keeping his covenant of love to a thousand generations of those who love him and keep his commandments."

Deuteronomy 7:9

Who is God faithful to, according to this Scripture? _____

_____

_____

_____

If you believe God is faithful, why is it so difficult to wait on Him? Why does the *meantime* seem as though God is being *mean?* _____

_____

_____

_____

What does living your best life mean to you? _____

_____

_____

_____

Read the story of the Shunammite woman in 2 Kings 4:8-37.

In the *meantime* of her story, how did her trial grow her faith? _____
_____
_____
_____

How can you emulate this woman's faith during your own trials? ___
_____
_____

"May the God of hope fill you with all joy and peace as you trust
in him, so that you may overflow with hope by the power of the
Holy Spirit."

Romans 15:13

According to this Scripture, what happens when you trust God? ____
_____
_____

How can you begin each day with a hopeful heart? _____
_____
_____

Read John 15:1-17. Give some examples of what God promises to people
who surrender to Him. _____
_____
_____

"Before you were born I set you apart."

Jeremiah 1:5

"All the days ordained for me were written in your book before one of them came to be."

Psalm 139:16

These Scriptures clearly indicate that God has a purpose for your life. Describe what walking in your purpose looks like: _____

_____

_____

_____

_____

_____

_____

_____

_____

_____

_____

_____

_____

_____

_____

_____

_____

_____

_____

_____

_____

CHAPTER 5

The Time Is Now

I PERSIST IN DANGLING FROM this handrail, but something is happening. As usual, I hear voices. Satan tells me I have neither the strength nor the courage to regain my balance. He wants me to wear his brands, the lies that serve only to erode my self-worth. But the living, breathing Word of God drowns out those voices. I know who God says I am. By His grace, this chaos will not define me. He will use it to refine me. I begin to right myself.

I am so embarrassed. Everyone now knows the color of my underpants! Although they try to hide it, people are laughing at me, including my own family. Am I going to see myself the way they must, or will I focus on what God sees? Will I be like Eve and listen to what they say; or will I listen to God, like Sarah, Rahab, Deborah, Ruth, Esther, and Mary? I choose to listen to God and allow Him to use my trial for His glory.

Of course, that decision does not magically eliminate the present humiliation. How I wish I could go back in time and wear my bejeweled pink flip flops instead of my pink, cork-heeled platform shoes! Since that option is unavailable, I have a choice—angrily stomp out the door, carrying the weight of bitterness and regret and wondering why God allowed it to happen to me, blaming anything and anybody for my fall; or walk in His light straight to my seat, giving a magnificent high-five to the man who keeps asking if I am okay. I go for the high-five.

Finally seated, sore shoulder and bruised ego noted, I am caught up in silent, hysterical laughter, recalling the sight I made. This book did not come to be because I am famous, rich, or perfect—a fact upon which we can all now easily agree. Rather, I sometimes feel that life turns upside down, and I cannot seem to find myself among the chaos. I see myself as the world does and measure myself by what the enemy says, feeling as though I carry the weight of the world on my shoulders. I wonder if God sees, hears, or cares about me. This book was written because God's grace provided everything I needed to overcome a life that has been filled with chaos.

Your own inheritance will profoundly affect your life if you choose to accept and believe all God has for you in the middle of the chaos. Believe that God's grace provides everything you need to overcome trials, succeed in life, walk in peace, and live an abundant life. I have often heard people say, "Snow is a reminder of God's grace. It does not pick and choose where it falls. It covers everything." That thought perfectly describes your inheritance. God's beautiful grace covers every aspect of your life without picking or choosing who or how much it covers. It covers all, and it is yours if you choose to believe.

In 2 Corinthians 6:2, Paul says, "Now is the time of God's favor, now is the day of salvation." Stop doubting and making excuses. Believe who God says you are and stop wearing the enemy's brands.

When you do, you will stop caring what people think and comparing yourself to others; you will gain courage to say yes to God when He calls. You will stop standing behind closed doors and, instead, shake off what holds you back. You will prosper, knowing your worth cannot be measured. Have the courage to face darkness, knowing you walk in His light. Walk in peace and forgiveness, knowing your steps are ordered.

Live the best life possible, knowing God is faithful, both in His time and the meantime. Begin each day with a hopeful heart, live each day in sweet surrender, and believe each day in God's planned purpose for you. That, my friend, is the profound effect God's grace will have on your life. It is your godly inheritance.

It is *The Crown Effect.*

Pause For Reflection

Life is hard, and we all struggle. What do you struggle with the most today? _____

_____

_____

John 1:16 says, "Out of his fullness we have all received grace in place of grace already given." Your godly inheritance includes a never-ending flow of grace that covers you like snow. In 2 Corinthians 6:2, Paul says, "I tell you, now is the time of God's favor, now is the day of salvation." His grace is available to you. He loves you and wants to help, bless, teach, guide, and make you into all He created you to be. The time is now.

What changes will you make to live an abundant life in a chaotic world? For each statement that follows, list an area in which you can grow. Write a verse to claim or a habit you plan to make (or break!) in order to shake off the devil's brands, say yes to God, and take full advantage of *The Crown Effect:* _____

_____

_____

I will care more about *God's* opinion than man's in the area of _____

_____

_____.

Verse to claim:_____

Plan of action:_____

I will live under God's authority in the area of _____

_____

_____.

Verse to claim:_____

Plan of action:_____

I will say yes when God calls me to _____

_____

_____.

Verse to claim: _____

Plan of action: _____

I will let go of this that holds me back: _____

_____

_____.

Verse to claim: _____

Plan of action: _____

I will allow His light to shine through the darkness in: _____

_____

_____.

Verse to claim: _____

Plan of action: _____

I will trust God with _____

_____

_____

Verse to claim: _____

Plan of action: _____

I surrender my will to obey God in the area of _____

_____

_____.

Verse to claim: _____

Plan of action: _____

I trust His grace will profoundly affect my life in the area of _____

_____

_____.

Verse to claim: _____

Plan of action: _____

I will claim my godly inheritance by _____

_____

_____.

Verse to claim: _____

Plan of action: _____

ABOUT THE AUTHOR

KATHY VINTSON HAILS FROM INNER city Birmingham, Alabama. Raised by her grandparents, she learned the importance of trusting and believing in God for everything from a young age. Now retired from a career in education, she writes from a small corner desk that overlooks the lake, where she lives with her husband of more than thirty years. God has richly blessed her with the family she longed for as a child, and her walk is a living testimony of how God's grace provides all we need to overcome chaos and live an abundant life.

In addition to creating inspirational blog content, Kathy serves as a motivational speaker for women. She is passionate about encouraging women to claim all God has for them in order to live joyful, successful, abundant lives and to face each season in anticipation of God's plan for them. When she is not writing, Kathy spends time on the lake with her children and grandchildren.

Contact Information

Email: kathyvintson@gmail.com
Facebook Blog: www.facebook.com/KathyVintsonBlog
Instagram: www.instagram.com/kathy_vintson
Twitter: @KathyVintson

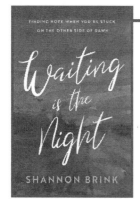

We all go through seasons of waiting, times when God just seems to have closed His ears to us and turned His back. During those seasons, it's easy to give up hope and lose heart. What can we learn from those times of waiting? Drawing from her own experiences and from the examples of God's people in the Bible who also experienced seasons of waiting, Shannon encourages the reader to hold on to the One Who created us. While waiting in the dark, cling to the Light.

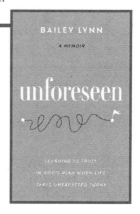

Bailey Lynn had her life perfectly planned. She thought she was on the path that God had preordained for her. But when her life took an unexpected turn, Bailey was left to question God's ability to dictate her life. In *Unforeseen: Learning to Trust in God's Plan When Life Takes Unexpected Turns*, Bailey shares how she learned to trust God with a future she had never planned. As she battled whether God's plans for her were truly as good as He had promised in His Word, Bailey began to see that His ways were definitely not like hers—they were better.

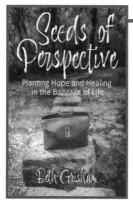

In *Seeds of Perspective*, women of all ages and walks of life willingly poured out their most difficult life situations as a personal sacrifice to help others process and find hope and healing in their own worst mistakes. They believe that remembering and sharing their stories awakens in each of us a deeper understanding of God's promise to redeem our lives for His glory and His purposes and to bring beauty from the ashes of our past.

Made in the USA
Columbia, SC
03 May 2024

9a4d6ed0-9e32-4234-87f8-5c23a92d8574R01